KWIK·SEW®
METHOD FOR SEWING
LINGERIE

by Kerstin Martensson

First Printing, May 1978
Second Printing, February 1979
Third Printing, May 1980
Fourth Printing, May 1981
Fifth Printing, December 1981

1

about the author

Kwik Sew Method for sewing lingerie is the tenth in a series of books on home sewing by Kerstin Martensson. Her previous best selling books have achieved worldwide success and popularity. The overwhelming acceptance of Kerstin Martensson's books can be attributed to their illustrated, easy-to-follow, step-by-step procedures. Over a half million copies of her books have been sold thus far. Many of these are being used by schools and colleges throughout the western world as sewing textbooks.

Kerstin Martensson is eminently qualified to write a book on lingerie. She made the first pattern produced by the KWIK-SEW Pattern Company. She learned pattern making and clothing construction at Goteborg's Stad Verkstadskola and Stockholm's Tillskarar Akademi in Sweden. Her simplified sewing techniques have been enthusiastically received by home sewers everywhere.

Since 1974, Kerstin has been the President of KWIK-SEW Pattern Company. She still personally supervises the Design and Pattern Departments of this company.

Kerstin's distinguished career as author, designer and lecturer includes numerous television and radio appearances. She has been credited with making the first film dealing exclusively with the techniques of sewing stretch fabrics at home. Her latest three films entitled "Anyone Can Sew Knit and Stretch Fabrics" have been extremely well received in the United States and Canada.

She has conducted training classes in all phases of sewing in the United States and Canada, as well as England, Germany and the Scandinavian countries.

All of Kerstin Martensson's books are carefully revised prior to each printing to keep them updated in the latest and newest sewing techniques. Previous books now available are:

It's Easy to Sew Swimwear
It's Easy to Sew Knit and Stretch Fabric
Sew for Baby - The Fun Way
Professional Pattern Alterations Made Easy
Kwik-Sew Method for Sewing Men's Wear

BOARD OF DIRECTORS

KWIK-SEW Pattern Co., Inc.

Fashion Illustrations by Judith Meyeraan

This is the tenth book written by Kerstin Martensson which has been fashion illustrated by Judith Meyeraan. Judith is employed by KWIK-SEW Pattern Co. as a fashion artist.

Judith Meyeraan attended the University of Minnesota and was graduated from Art Instruction, Inc.

TO CREATE is one of life's greatest satisfactions. Unfortunately, most women have little opportunity in today's world where everything is mass-produced and where everything and everyone tends to look alike.

However, creating ones own lingerie opens the door to let every woman be creative — as creative as she wishes, for lingerie, more than anything else, gives her the opportunity to use her imagination. It is not by accident that the idea of sewing lingerie at home has swept the country — women from all stations in life have joined in this fascinating field of sewing.

Sewing lingerie is much simpler and faster than you can imagine, but in addition you get an opportunity to let your imagination run wild with the use of fancy laces and soft sheer fabric.

A beautiful frilly peignoir of the sheerest nylon makes a perfect gift. You may wish to include matching slippers, or a matching bouffant curler bonnet. Instructions for making these as well as other gift items are included in this book. Sewing lingerie not only includes sewing on soft sheer fabrics, but it is now possible for you to make your own girdles and bras as all types of lingerie fabrics, laces and other supplies are now available to everyone.

We hope that this book will show how easy it is for you to be creative.

contents

general sewing information

Nylon was one of the original "test-tube" fabrics. It was first introduced commercially in 1938 as a fabric for stockings. Since that time, scientists have discovered thousands of additional uses for this material. We will, however, consider its use only as a lingerie fabric.

Nylon is especially suited for lingerie fabrics as the fibers are elastic and extremely strong. In addition, they return rapidly to their original shape. Nylon also washes easily and dries quickly. These last two advantages are very important for lingerie garments.

Nylon is a brand name, not a generic name, but the word nylon is so common it can be considered to be a generic name. Lingerie nylon comes in endless varieties which include various elastics, laces, and ribbons as well as the following fabrics.

NYLON TRICOT

This is the most common nylon lingerie fabric and it comes in various weights depending upon what type of garment the fabric will be used for.

40 denier is heavyweight, 30 denier is medium weight; both of these can be used for single layer gowns, robes, slips, panties and pajamas. 20 denier is lightweight and can be used for panties and two layer gowns.

NYLON SHEER

This is an extremely light and sheer fabric, it is 15 denier and it is usually used as a second layer over tricot to give a softer, more feminine look. An example of this would be the overlayer on a nightgown or peignoir. While nylon sheer gives the impression of being very delicate, it is actually extremely strong. It can also be used for trimming and binding and as a backing for lace.

CREPE TRICOT

Crepe tricot is usually between nylon sheer and nylon tricot in weight. It has a frosty surface which helps you to identify it. It can be used for panties, slips, nightgowns and peignoirs.

SATINIZED TRICOT

This is a type of tricot which looks like satin on the right side. This tricot is very often used for nightgowns and peignoirs.

BRUSHED NYLON

This is a type of nylon that resembles flannel as it has a soft "feel". It is warmer than nylon tricot. This is the reason it is very suitable for gowns and robes. Because it is warm, it is very often used for children's sleepwear.

QUILTED NYLON

This is a type of fabric mainly used for robes. It is very warm as it consists of two layers of fabric with a fiber fill between the layers. Stitches are sewn on the fabric, usually following a design, to keep the fill in place.

STABILIZED NYLON

This fabric differs from other nylon fabrics in the fact that it does not stretch. It is mostly used for slips, either full or half. The advantage of using this fabric for slips is that it does not cling to the garment - this is an especially good quality when wearing knits. In addition, stabilized nylon does not build up static electricity.

Regardless of the type of fabric, nylon is very easy to care for. In addition to its quick drying quality, it requires little or no ironing. However, if it is necessary to iron the garment, never use a hot iron. Set your iron for a temperature of 250 - 275°F. A hotter iron than this might cause the fabric to wrinkle or even melt. It is actually best, whenever possible, to hang up the garment to dry and this should almost eliminate ironing as nylon is very wrinkle resistant and tends to revert to its original shape.

Whenever possible, use nylon for the entire garment and it will be much easier to care for. Remember, never use cotton thread for nylon garments. When washed, the thread may shrink which will cause puckering of the seams.

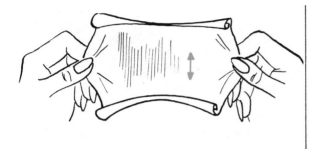

It is very important to determine the right and wrong side of nylon fabric. This is very difficult when using nylon tricot or nylon sheer as both sides look almost alike. This is especially true when you have cut out the pattern; however, any mistake will show up when the garment is completed.

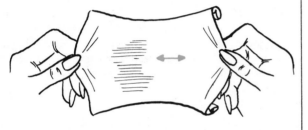

To determine the right side, cut the fabric across the grain and stretch it. The cut edge will always roll to the right side. Remember that the greatest stretch is across the grain. If you stretch the fabric with the grain, it will curl to the wrong side.

Having introduced you to the principle fabrics we will be working with in lingerie sewing, we would like to give you a very brief description of the man-made fibers, such as nylon, and their chief characteristics, as they do differ considerably from natural fibers such as cotton, wool, and silk. These chemically synthesized fibers fall into several large groups, four of which we will briefly mention here.

The main group of fibers used in lingerie sewing is the polyamide group. The most common brand name for this group is Nylon. Other names are Crepeset, Enka Nylon, Girlon (Switzerland), Nyfil (Mexico), Perlon (Germany), Rilsan (Italy), Amilan (Japan), and Antron. One of the main characteristics of these fibers is their ability to return to their original shape. They dry quickly and are very strong. As with all synthetic fabrics, wash them often and do not permit them to get too dirty. When washing nylon, try to separate the colored garments from the white as there is a tendency for the white nylon to pick up the colors from the colored garments. Do not wash nylon, or any other man-made fiber in hot water. Do not dry nylon in direct sunlight as it tends to turn yellow. However, if this does happen, nylon is easy to dye and when dyed gives the appearance of a brand new garment. To identify nylon using the flame test, remember that it melts very slowly with a small flame, leaving a hard, round, grey ash.

Another important group of fibers is the polyester group which includes Dacron. Dacron actually is not the name of a fiber but it is a brand name. The fibers are polyester. Other brand names for this fiber are Fortrel, Kodel, Vycron, Encron, Terylene and Trevira. These various brands differ especially according to how they react to heat. Always try your iron on a piece of scrap fabric to determine how much heat the fabric can stand. All of these polyester fabrics are quick-drying; they resist wrinkling; have excellent resiliency, and require little care. To identify a polyester fabric, burn a small piece. It should burn slowly and melt, leaving a hard, black, round ash.

The third group of fabrics is made from Polyakryl - known also as acrylic. The most common name is Orlon. This particular brand is very soft and resembles fine wool. The difference is that Orlon has a tendency to pill. It is much easier to care for than wool. If you have a garment which has pilled (small knots on the surface), use a razor to shave the garment and it will be as good as new. Other familiar brand names for this group are Acrilan, Creslan, Dralon, Dynel, Courtelle. The reaction to flame is the same as the polyester group. As Orlon is difficult to tell apart from wool, remember that wool smells like burnt hair, burns with a flame, and the ash is very soft.

The final group is the Elastomeric fibers. This is the Spandex fiber, of which Lycra is the most familiar trade name. Others include Vyrene, Spandelle and Glospan. These fibers are used in manufacturing fabrics where stretch is required and have the distinct advantage over rubber in that they are lightweight, have high-holding power and good resistance to abrasion, chlorine bleaches and machine laundering.

This information is for pure fabrics only - not for blends. There are so many possibilities for various blends that we could not possibly list all their characteristics. This is especially true when you consider the endless possibilities of blending man-made with natural fibers. Many women believe that a blend of - say Dacron and cotton - is not as good as all cotton, or all Dacron. This is not true. A man's shirt of 65 percent Dacron and 35 per cent cotton is much better than a shirt of either all cotton or all Dacron. The reason for this is that the Dacron will not absorb moisture, but it holds its shape and resists wrinkling. The cotton will absorb moisture, but it wrinkles. The combination of these two fibers gives a shirt that will be wrinkle resistant and also will absorb moisture.

It is always wise to become familiar with the fabrics with which you are working, their properties and the best way to care for them.

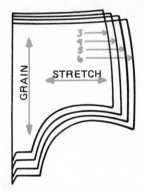

PATTERNS

When working with knit and stretch fabrics, including lingerie, it is very important to use patterns designed especially for these fabrics.

If you use a pattern designed for non-stretch fabric, you will end up with a garment which is too large for you. All the patterns referred to in this book are made by KWIK-SEW. KWIK-SEW has patterns which are designed for both stretch and non-stretch fabrics.

There is one exception, when you are using a pattern for robes and gowns. You can use a pattern for either stretch or non-stretch fabric. However, if you are using a pattern which calls for a 5/8" (1.5 cm) seam allowance and you are constructing a garment using nylon tricot, you should cut away the seam allowance to give you a ¼"(6 mm) seam allowance.

Included in the back of this book is a master pattern which can be used for both stretch and non-stretch fabric. How to change these master patterns to obtain very interesting variations is explained in Section 5.

Before you buy the fabric, select the pattern as each pattern indicates what type of fabric is necessary and how much fabric is required. These patterns also indicate how much lace is needed, what notions are required, etc.

KWIK-SEW Patterns have at least three sizes included in each envelope and each size is marked in a different color, making it very easy for you to cut out the correct size.

Complete easy-to-follow instructions are included with each pattern as well as instructions on how to properly set your sewing machine so that it will sew these fabrics. Even if you are making your first lingerie garment or if you are an inexperienced sewer, you should have no difficulty in obtaining a very professional looking garment.

KWIK-SEW patterns are sized using the United States Government sizing specifications. To be certain that you are obtaining the correct size, check the sizes on the back of the pattern envelope and compare these with the actual body measurements. A certain amount of ease is included in the patterns. The amount of ease varies according to the design of the pattern, the style and type of the garment, and the type of fabric to be used. For example, a pattern for non-stretch fabric includes more ease than a pattern for stretch fabric. The pattern pieces for a girdle are actually smaller than your body measurements. This is necessary so that the girdle will fit properly.

When you are using patterns designed for stretch fabric, it is important to use the fabric with the correct degree of stretch. To determine the correct amount of stretch, use the stretch chart. Fold the fabric double and gently stretch the fabric. Do not stretch the fabric so tight that the fabric rolls excessively. This is also a good time to check the fabric for recovery. If the fabric does not go back to its original shape after being stretched, it will probably mean that the fabric will sag and stretch out of shape when the garment is worn.

STRETCH

Nylon tricot and nylon sheer should stretch 25% across the grain.

5" of knit fabric should stretch	to here →

Power net should stretch 70% across the grain.

4" of power net should stretch	to here ⟹

Single knit, double knit and knit and stretch fabric should stretch 18% across the grain.

5" of knit fabric should stretch	to here →

Many lingerie patterns are marked small, medium, large and extra large. Compare your body measurements with the chart to determine which size you require for a proper fit.

LADIES' BODY MEASUREMENTS

	Small			Medium		Large		Extra Large	
Size	6	8	10	12	14	16	18	20	22
Bust	32½" (83 cm)	34" (86 cm)	35½" (90 cm)	37" (94 cm)	38½" (98 cm)	40" (102 cm)	41½" (106 cm)	43" (110 cm)	45" (114 cm)
Waist	23½" (59 cm)	24½" (62 cm)	25½" (65 cm)	27" (68 cm)	28½" (72 cm)	30¼" (77 cm)	32¼" (82 cm)	34" (86 cm)	36½" (93 cm)
Hip	34" (86 cm)	35½" (90 cm)	37" (94 cm)	38½" (98 cm)	40" (102 cm)	41¾" (106 cm)	43¼" (110 cm)	45" (115 cm)	47" (120 cm)
Back Length	15½" (39.5 cm)	15¾" (40 cm)	16" (41 cm)	16¼" (41.5 cm)	16½" (42 cm)	16¾" (42.5 cm)	17" (43 cm)	17" (43 cm)	17" (43 cm)

MISS JUNIOR TEENS BODY MEASUREMENT

Size	5	7	9	11
Bust	31½" (80 cm)	33" (84 cm)	34½" (88 cm)	36¼" (92 cm)
Waist	23" (58 cm)	23½" (60 cm)	24½" (62 cm)	25½" (65 cm)
Hip	33" (84 cm)	34½" (88 cm)	36¼" (92 cm)	37¾" (96 cm)
Back Length	15¼" (39 cm)	15½" (39.5 cm)	15¾" (40 cm)	16" (40.5 cm)

QUEEN SIZE

Bust Size	48	51	54	57
Bust	48" (122 cm)	51" (130 cm)	54" (137 cm)	57" (145 cm)
Waist	40" (102 cm)	43" (109 cm)	46" (117 cm)	49" (124 cm)
Hip	50" (127 cm)	53" (135 cm)	56" (142 cm)	59" (150 cm)
Back Length	17" (43 cm)	17¼" (44 cm)	17½" (44.5 cm)	17¾" (45 cm)

Before cutting the garment, check to make sure that the length is correct. This is the most common adjustment on any pattern. If any major adjustment has to be made on the pattern and you are not sure how to make the adjustment, refer to the book "PROFESSIONAL PATTERN ALTERATIONS MADE EASY", published by KWIK-SEW Pattern Co., Inc.

KWIK-SEW patterns are carried by most leading fabric stores in the United States, Canada and Australia. If your store does not have the patterns, they can obtain them for you.

CUTTING

As most lingerie fabric is made from synthetic fibers, you will find that your scissors will become dull quicker than when cutting natural fibers. It is very important to have a clean cut so make sure you start out with a pair of sharp scissors and if they should become dull, get them sharpened as soon as possible. Never, we repeat, never use your sewing scissors for cutting anything else - especially paper! Cutting paper dulls the scissors very quickly.

Place the fabric double, right side to right side, before you start cutting. Make sure the fold is along the grain in order to insure a proper fit. Try to follow the same thread across the entire fold. As nylon fabric is stretchy and slippery, try to keep the fabric on top of the table and not hanging down as this will tend to pull it out of shape and the pieces will not be identical with the pattern. This is especially true when cutting out a maxi-length garment, as very few of us have a table large enough for these garments. As a solution, we suggest that you spread the fabric and the pattern pieces on a carpeted floor. Notice how the nylon is easier to work with when the surface is not slippery. For smaller patterns, bear this in mind and place a tablecloth on the table before cutting. If you have a cutting board, use it as the surface is usually not as slippery as a table.

Regardless of the garment you are making, always be sure to follow the arrows on the pattern pieces to make sure you have the grain and stretch of the fabric in the right directions. This is especially important when you are working with stretch fabric, as the stretch must always go around the body. For example, if you are making a pair of panties and you have the fabric stretch going up and down instead of around the body, you will not be able to get the panties on.

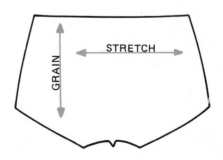

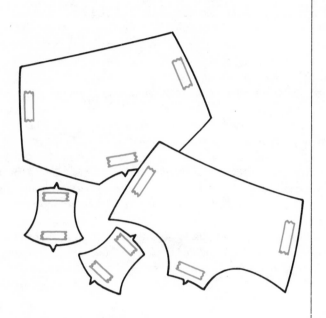

As nylon is a very tough fiber, it is important that you use very fine pins with sharp points when you pin the pattern to the fabric. Some people prefer to use weights to hold the pattern pieces in place. Ash trays, cups, etc. will do very nicely as long as they keep the pattern steady on the fabric.

So that you do not mix up the pieces of fabric, always mark them. We recommend using transparent tape. Place a small piece on the wrong side of the fabric marking the side seams, waistline, etc. This tape has a dull finish which you can write on. Always use a pencil as a ball point pen could spot the garment and these spots are very difficult to wash out. This tape can also be used for basting and has many other useful applications. As you read on you will find how this is done, plus you will discover many other short-cuts that rely on this tape. Be careful when you are using transparent tape, if you are using velour or other fabric with a similar surface, as it may mark the fabric. Try the tape on a piece of scrap fabric before you use it.

Don't throw away the fabric you have left over after you have finished cutting out the garment. In lingerie, more than in any other fabric, these pieces can be used as trim for other garments or they can be used to make very interesting and attractive small gift items.

SIZE
10 OR 11

Before you start sewing, take a small piece of scrap fabric, double the fabric and sew a straight stitch. If the seam has a tendency to pucker or skip stitches, this is usually caused by a dull or bent needle. This may not show when sewing on a heavier type of fabric. The most important rule to follow when sewing on nylon is to use a fine and sharp needle - size 10 or 11 can be used. You should always bear in mind that nylon is a very tough fabric and it has a tendency to dull the needle.

Even though you may start out with a new sharp needle you will find that you have to change the needle more often than when sewing with natural fabrics. For some unknown reason, some women think that you have to use a ball point needle when sewing lingerie. This is not correct except when using high-speed power machines. For the regular home type sewing machine, you should use a modified ball point needle. This is the standard needle supplied with all good European sewing machines.

If you have changed the needle and the seam still puckers, you may have to adjust your thread tension. The perfect thread tension results when the top and bottom tension are exactly equal and the knot is buried in the fabric and cannot be seen. This is easily done in heavy soft fabric such as felt or wool. But nylon and most lingerie fabric is very thin and you will usually see the knot on both sides. The best rule to follow is to adjust the tensions so that the stitch appears the same on both sides. See diagram. Try only to adjust the top tension as this is easier to do on all sewing machines but in some cases, you will have to adjust both the top and bottom tensions.

When sewing on stretch fabric, it is very important to use the correct pressure on the presser foot. The most up-to-date machines can all be adjusted.

This is usually a simple adjustment and can be accomplished by turning a dial. For most lingerie fabric use the regular pressure except for girdle fabric which requires a heavier pressure in order to reduce the possibility of skipped stitches.

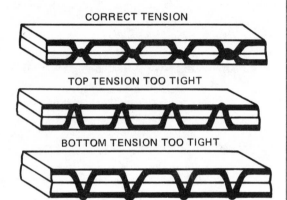

CORRECT TENSION

TOP TENSION TOO TIGHT

BOTTOM TENSION TOO TIGHT

THREAD

The proper thread is very important when sewing lingerie. As synthetic fabric stretches, you should use a thread that also stretches with the fabric and returns to normal when the "stretch" is relaxed. There are many threads that do this; however, some have very obvious disadvantages. An example of this is nylon monofilament thread. (This is very similar to the monofilament fishing line used with spin tackle.) The trouble with this thread is that it is very stiff and greatly increases the possibility of skipped stitches. Unless cotton thread has been preshrunk, you generally end up with puckered seams after the garment has been washed.

There are many excellent synthetic threads on the market that have been developed especially for sewing with stretch fabrics. These threads are color-fast and extremely strong. This strength is very important, for example, when constructing girdles and bras. The advantage of these threads is that they have "controlled stretch". This is essential when sewing stretch fabric. In addition, they are very fine threads which is necessary for sewing sheer fabric. Yet, because of their great strength, you can also use them for sewing ski pants where it is very important to have a thread which is extremely strong. These threads can also be used in all types of sewing as they are fade-resistant and will not shrink. They come in a variety of colors. Regardless of the type of thread you are using, always be sure to use the same thread on the top of the sewing machine as you use on the bobbin.

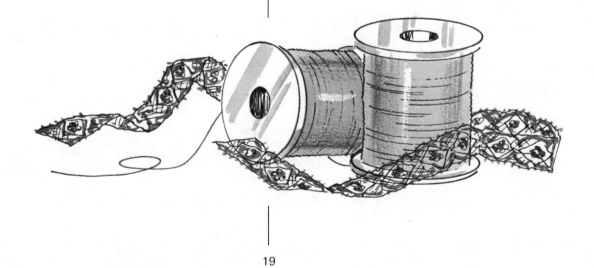

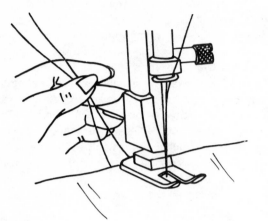

As lingerie fabric is very fine and soft you will find it much easier to start a seam if you lower the needle into the fabric holding both the top and bottom thread in your hand behind the presser foot. As the machine starts to sew, slowly pull these threads towards the rear of the machine. This will tend to help the machine feed the material and eliminate the tendency of the material to bunch up under the presser foot. As a general rule, never back-stitch when sewing lingerie as you will find it extremely difficult to eliminate bunching regardless of the type of sewing machine you may be using.

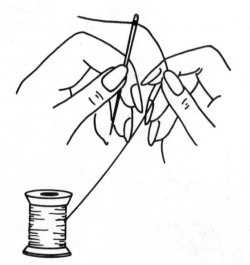

Almost all lingerie sewing is done by using a sewing machine. However, in some cases, you have to sew a few stitches by hand and the following should always be kept in mind. All synthetic thread is manufactured from synthetic fibers and these fibers tend to revert to their original shape. It is very important when sewing by hand that you always thread the needle from the end coming off the spool. If you do not follow this procedure, you will end up with small knots in the thread (and fraying). Always remember to use a very fine needle as it slips easier through the tough nylon fabric.

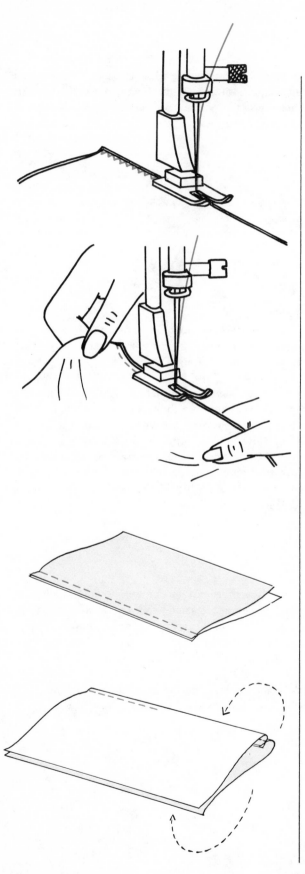

SEAMS

As nylon tricot and nylon sheer do not ravel, you can use a very narrow seam allowance. The most professional looking garment can be sewn by using a narrow zigzag stitch.

Many of the KWIK-SEW patterns call for 1/8″ (3 mm) seam allowance. When sewing a seam, try to sew on the edge of the fabric so that the needle barely misses the edge of the fabric on the right hand swing. (Always keep the fabric to the left of the needle.)

If you do not have a zigzag machine, you should stretch the fabric slightly while sewing. Still sew the seam using 1/8″ (3 mm) seam allowance.

If you are using a straight stitch, to obtain a more professional look, we recommend that you make a French seam. For a French seam you must place the wrong sides of the fabric together and make the first seam on the right side. If you need a larger seam allowance, add ¼″ (6 mm).

Then turn the garment the wrong side out and make a second stitch far enough in so that the raw edges do not show.

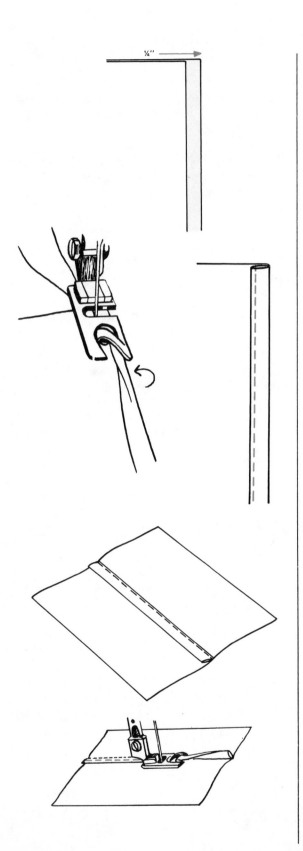

Another technique for making a French seam is done with a hemmer. Almost all sewing machines come with various width hemmers. Do not use the narrow hemmer which is used for rolled hems.

So that the French seam does not appear too bulky as you sew both layers together at the same time, the bottom layer should extend ¼" (6 mm) to the right.

Fold this bottom layer to the left as you slip it into the hemmer. It is easier to start the fabric through the hemmer if you turn the machine by hand and make two stitches in the fabric. Now, use the threads to pull the fabric away from you. After a few stitches the machine will take over and move the fabric towards the rear of the machine. As you sew, the hemmer will fold the fabric and give you a finished French seam.

A flat felled seam is not as commonly used in lingerie sewing but by using the same hemmer and the same technique, you can obtain this seam. The only difference is that this requires one more operation. After you have sewn the French seam, pull the fabric apart so that it is lying flat.

Pull the seam up into the hemmer and the hemmer will sew the second seam so that it lies flat.

ELASTIC

In most fabric stores that handle lingerie fabric, you can obtain special lingerie elastic. This elastic comes in a great variety of colors and in various widths according to what it is to be used for. The most common width for use around the leg openings is ¼'' (6 mm) wide. For use around the waist, it should be ½'' (1.3 cm) wide. Lingerie elastic has a softer stretch than regular elastic and usually has one ''fancy'' edge.

If your store does not handle lingerie elastic, you can use regular elastic and we will show you later on in this section how this regular elastic can be used in lingerie sewing.

There is a different type of lingerie elastic which is used for bras and girdles. The use of these elastics is explained in the section covering girdles and bras.

Almost all women have a different idea as to how tight the elastic should fit around the waist and the legs. A good rule to remember is to have the elastic 4'' (10 cm) smaller than the waist or leg measurement. This can be adjusted if you prefer a tighter fit or if you like to have less pressure.

As lingerie elastic comes with one ''fancy'' edge, you can either have this edge at the bottom or top. However, we have found that it is better to have the ''fancy'' edge facing the fabric as this edge tends to ruffle when washed and this gives the garment a used appearance.

It is often very difficult to tell the right side from the wrong side when using lingerie elastic. This is not important. The important thing to remember is to make sure that the same side is always on the right side throughout the garment.

Whenever you have to use elastic, you usually start out by sewing the correct length in a circle and this can be done in different ways as follows:

Right side to right side using a straight stitch ¼'' (6 mm) from the edge.

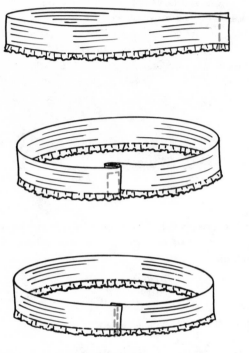

Another method is to fold each edge under ¼'' (6 mm), hide the seam allowance and sew all around.

Most ready-to-wear garments merely place the elastic so that the ends overlap approximately ¼'' (6 mm). Sew them together securely.

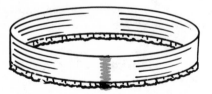

Still another method is to place the ends of the elastic edge to edge. Sew the ends together using a slightly wider than medium zigzag and a short stitch length.

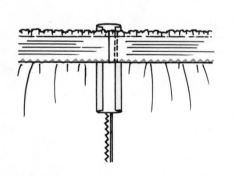

To hide this seam when you apply the elastic, use either ready-made satin ribbon ½'' (1.3 cm) wide or cut a piece of nylon tricot along the grain 1'' (2.5 cm) wide and 2'' (5 cm) long.

If you are using nylon tricot, fold the edges under the long way ¼'' (6 mm) on each side. When you apply the elastic, place this strip under the elastic where the elastic is sewn together.

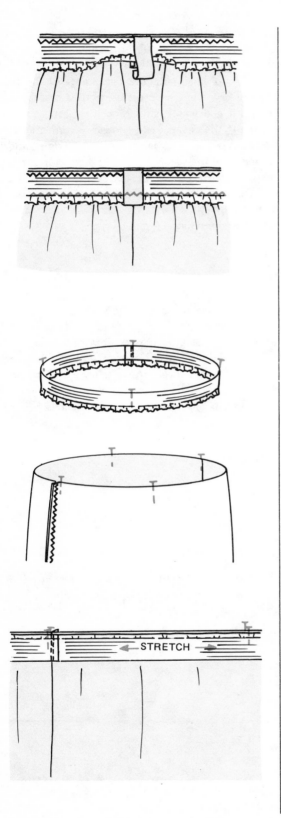

After you sew the elastic onto the garment (through all three layers) you turn the elastic to the right side, cover the seam in the elastic with the tricot and tuck the ends under the elastic before you sew the second seam on the elastic. If you do not cover the ends of the elastic using the above procedure, the ends of the elastic will tend to ruffle when washed and this will give you a rather messy looking seam.

When you are applying a circular form of elastic, the easiest method regardless if it be the waist or the legs, is to divide the circle of elastic by four and mark each fourth with a pin.

Divide the opening, such as the top of a half slip, in the same manner.

Always make sure the elastic seam is on one side seam when it is used in the waist. For leg openings it should always be on the outside as it is very uncomfortable to have this seam on the inside of the leg. When applying elastic to the openings, match the pins, and, as you sew on the elastic, stretch the elastic between the pins. This gives you the same amount of stretch all around the opening.

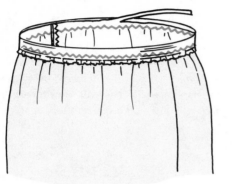

The fastest method for sewing the elastic onto the garment, but not necessarily the most professional looking, is to place the wrong side of the elastic on the right side of the garment, edge to edge, with the fancy edge of the elastic facing down. Sew the elastic on by using a zigzag stitch, medium width and length, stretching the elastic to fit the fabric. Cut off the excess seam allowance from the wrong side as close as possible to the stitches. If you do not have a zigzag stitch, sew the seam twice with a straight stitch for greater strength. Regardless of the type of stitch, try to sew between the rubber thread in the elastic. If you do not do this there will be a tendency for the elastic to break when stretched or washed.

The most professional looking method is to place the wrong side of the elastic on the wrong side of the fabric with the fancy edge of the elastic facing up. Sew the elastic on with a narrow zigzag stitch or a straight stitch on the lower edge of the elastic. Do not forget to stretch the elastic both in front and in back of the presser foot while sewing. Trim off any extra seam allowance close to the stitches.

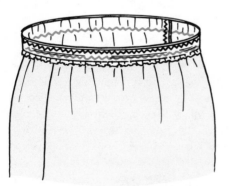

Turn the elastic to the right side, sew a second seam close to the fancy edge, but not on it. Again, remember to stretch the elastic.

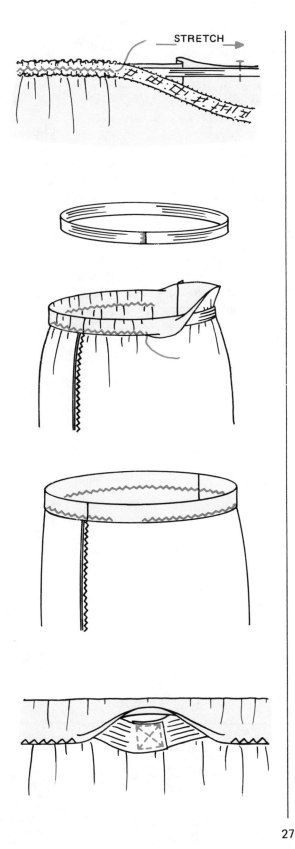

If you cannot obtain lingerie elastic, you can use regular elastic. Just remember that it is more comfortable to have a narrow elastic around the leg openings. For the leg openings in children's panties, you can use a very narrow elastic 1/8" (3 mm) wide; stretch the elastic while sewing and over the elastic place a narrow strip of lace. Sew all three layers together in one operation with a zigzag stitch and you will have a very attractive finish around the leg openings. If you feel it is difficult to sew all three layers at the same time, you can sew the elastic on first and then the lace in a second operation.

Regular elastic can be used for the waist but it is necessary that you have a casing. Regular elastic is much harder than lingerie elastic and in this case, the elastic should be only one or two inches less than your waist measurement. We suggest you measure around your waist and use as much elastic as feels comfortable. Overlap the ends by a half inch and sew the ends together.

Place the elastic on the wrong side and fold the material over the elastic, tucking the edge under the elastic. Sew a seam to make the casing. If you use a very narrow zigzag stitch, try to have the needle straddle the edge of the fabric. Be sure not to catch the elastic with the stitches. If you are using a straight stitch, it is important that you stretch the fabric as you sew. If you do not do this, there is a possibility that the seam will break when the fabric is stretched.

If you prefer, you can make the casing first and then insert the elastic. Just remember to leave a 1" (2.5 cm) opening for inserting the elastic. After you insert the elastic, sew the ends securely together and then close the opening.

LACE

Many women believe that lace is difficult to work with. This is probably because lace looks expensive and exclusive. Actually, it is very easy and simpler to apply than it is to make a straight hem. Not only is it easy, but the application of lace really gives you an opportunity to use your imagination and be creative.

Lace comes in an almost endless variety of shapes, sizes, colors and fibers. Always keep in mind to use lace made of nylon when sewing lingerie. It is not necessary to have the same color lace as the fabric you are sewing it on. In many cases you can get a much more striking effect by using a contrasting color. Or, you can use the same basic color but in a darker or lighter shade. Beige and brown go very well together. Another example is white lace on almost any color. The width of the lace depends both upon your individual preference and the type of garment you are constructing. Usually you should use a narrow lace when applying it to children's lingerie or nightgowns.

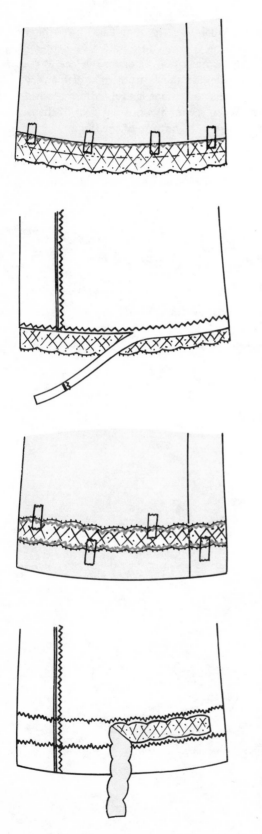

The following technique can be followed wherever the lace will be used for the finished edge of a garment. This is usually the hemline.

Place the lace on the right side of the fabric overlapping approximately 1'' (2.5 cm) or more. Do not apply very close to the edge of the fabric as it is much more difficult to sew. Instead of using pins to hold the lace in place, here is a great time to use transparent tape. This is a much easier method as the pins tend to get tangled in the lace. Place small strips of the tape at cross angles to the lace. You can sew over this tape without the needle getting "sticky". The best stitch to use when sewing lace is a narrow zigzag stitch, but do not set the length too close together. Remove the tape when you have finished sewing the seam. Trim away the excess fabric on the back side.

If you wish to insert lace, place the lace where you wish to have it and tape the lace in place. Use the method described above to sew on the lace. Make sure that you sew both edges of the lace. If the lace has scallops or if the edge is uneven be sure to follow the scallops on the outside of the design to obtain a much more professional looking appearance.

Now cut away the fabric under the lace but be very careful that you do not cut the lace.

It is not always necessary to cut away the fabric under the lace; you merely sew the lace on both edges. Some women prefer this method as the garments are stronger and others do not like to have the lace next to the skin, especially when lace is used on a pair of panties.

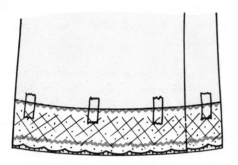

Sometimes when you are using lace of a different color or shade than the tricot, you obtain a very interesting effect if the tricot is not cut away under the lace. If you are using this technique for the bottom of a garment, you should make sure that the tricot is even with the bottom edge of the lace. When sewing the bottom edge of the lace, sew ¼'' (6 mm) up from the bottom of the lace.

When you trim the tricot as close as possible to the stitches, you get a much neater looking edge as any uneven cuts will be covered by the lace.

30

slips

No woman seems to have enough slips. At the last moment we always seem to be looking for a special color to go with a particular dress or skirt. This is especially true for lighter weight fabrics where the color of the slip shows through. Slips are so easy to construct that this should no longer present a problem. This is especially true for half-slips. The full slip is a little more complicated to make, but after you have made one or two, you will find that even these present no problems. Even the style where the panties and slip are constructed as one garment, is very simple to make. This is an item very popular with teenagers. The slip and panties are one unit. The advantage of this is that only one layer of elastic is necessary, thus reducing a ridge which is quite noticeable under light summer dresses.

We are going to start with a half-slip as this is the easiest lingerie item to make. Some of the techniques of inserting elastic and applying lace can be used on almost all garments. The best results are obtained if you use medium weight nylon tricot. Lace is not necessary, but it adds a certain amount of "feminine" touch and permits you to create many interesting variations.

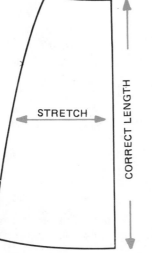

STRETCH

CORRECT LENGTH

Place the fabric right side together and cut out the pattern. Before cutting, make sure that the stretch goes around the body and that the slip is approximately 2" (5 cm) wider than your hip measurement. Check the length of the slip and take into consideration the width of any lace you might wish to add to the bottom. When sewing the side seams, the easiest method is to use a small zigzag stitch. Refer to Section 1 for seams.

If you want a bottom edge without lace, fold the hem to the wrong side either very narrow or as wide as desired, depending upon which you believe looks the nicest. Tuck in the raw edge and sew with a small zigzag stitch on the edge, or use a plain straight stitch.

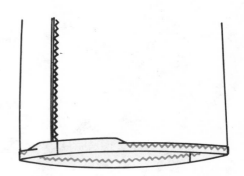

You can also use some of the decorative stitches on your sewing machine. For a variation, you can scallop the bottom edge with a blind hem stitch.

If you wish to use lace as a finished edge at the bottom of the slip, the easiest method is to sew only one side seam. Then, place slip flat with the right side up. You can use any width of lace that you desire. Cut the length of the lace so that it is long enough to go all across the bottom of the slip. Make sure that the top of the lace is equal-distance down from top of the slip so that when you sew the second side seam, the lace will meet exactly.

Be sure that the ends of the lace match at the side seam. Tape the lace onto the tricot with a few pieces of transparent tape.

Sew the top edge of the lace to the tricot. If this edge is scalloped or straight, follow the edge of the lace when you sew it on.

Trim the extra tricot under the lace as close as possible to the seam, being very careful not to cut the lace.

If you do not wish the lace to hang freely, sew a seam at bottom edge of the lace, be sure that the bottom edge of the lace is even with the bottom edge of the tricot. Sew the seam ¼'' (6 mm) from the edge of the lace. Trim the excess tricot on the inside close to the stitches.

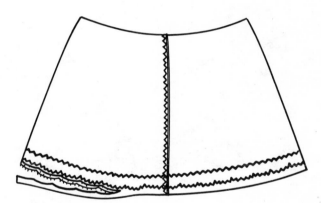

Sew the second side seam, remembering to make sure that the lace matches at this seam.

As there is more than one way to apply the waist elastic, refer to Section 1 for details.

33

For an invisible seam in your hemline lace, sew both the side seams of the slip. Tape the lace to the bottom edge of the slip, extend the lace on one side seam approximately 2″ (5 cm); overlap the ends of the lace. Sew a seam at the top edge of the lace. Trim the tricot close to the stitches on the inside.

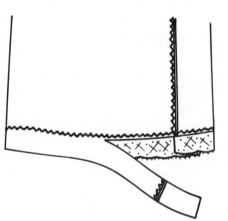

On right side of lace, sew a narrow zigzag seam through the two thicknesses of lace, following the design in the lace.

Trim excess lace from right and wrong sides, as close as possible to the stitches.

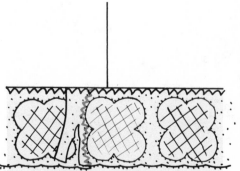

LACE INSERT

A lace insert makes a very attractive variation and it is very simple, as you apply the lace at the same time as you hem the bottom edge. Sew one side seam. Fold a 1½″ (3.8 cm) hem to the wrong side and tape the edges in place.

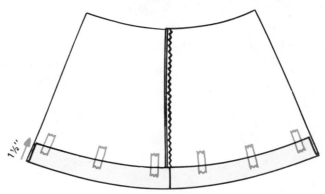

Now, on the right side of the fabric, place any width of lace 1″ (2.5 cm) up from the folded hemline. Tape in place.

Sew both edges of the lace, using a narrow zigzag stitch or straight stitch. One edge of lace is sewn through two layers of tricot; the other edge is sewn through one layer of tricot. Trim tricot under lace from wrong side close to stitches. Sew the other side seam. Make sure that the lace matches at the side seam.

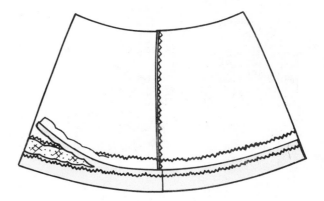

You can obtain a very interesting effect by using lace inserts of various widths. Sew some strips of lace, making sure that there is some tricot between the strips. Trim away the tricot under the lace.

HEMLINE LACE WITH SLIT

When constructing a slip with a slit, sew both side seams. Cut a length of lace long enough to go around hemline of slip plus approximately 17" (43 cm) for an 8" (20 cm) slit. Fold the lace in half. As the back and the front of a half slip are identical, you can very easily get the scallops in the lace matching at the slit, if you fold the lace exactly in the middle of a scallop. Place this point at one side seam.

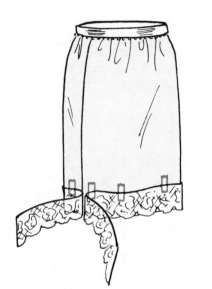

Tape lace to bottom of slip leaving 8½″ (22 cm) ends at side seams. The excess lace will be used for the slit.

Miter the lace at the bottom edge and fold as shown in the diagram to form the slit. The bottom edge of the lace should be towards the slip. Tape the lace in place.

Arrange lace at the top of the slit either with a straight line or cut the lace at an angle. Fold under the top edge of the lace ¼″ (6 mm) to get a nicer finish. Do the same on the other side of the slit.

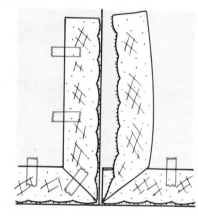
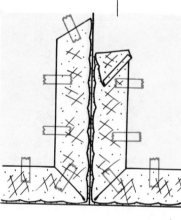
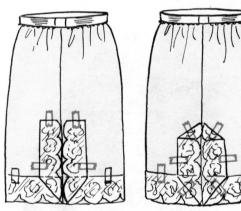

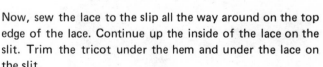

Now, sew the lace to the slip all the way around on the top edge of the lace. Continue up the inside of the lace on the slit. Trim the tricot under the hem and under the lace on the slit.

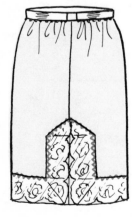
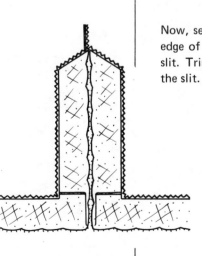

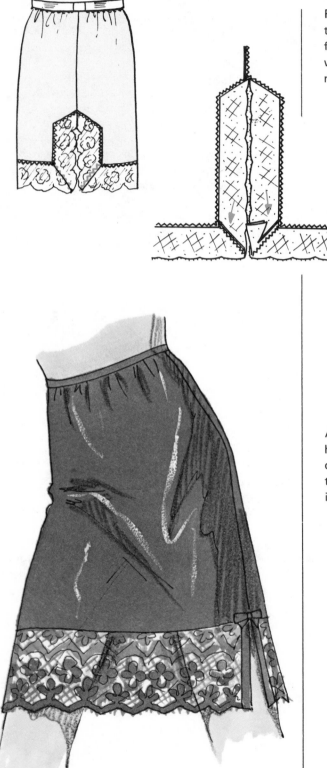

Finish the angle in the lace at the bottom of the slit by topstitching with a zigzag stitch. Trim off the excess lace from wrong side. In order to reinforce the top of the slip where the lace joins, sew a few stitches or sew on a small ribbon bow.

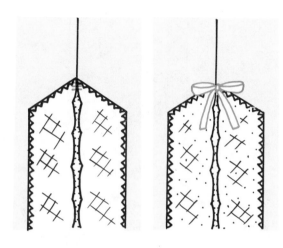

Another method of finishing the slit, if you just want to have the slit as wide as the bottom lace, is to sew the lace on and leave it open at one side seam. Cut away any excess tricot underneath. This makes a very attractive finish and it is very simple if you follow these directions.

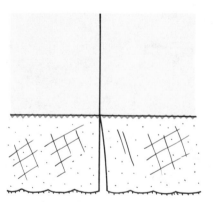

38

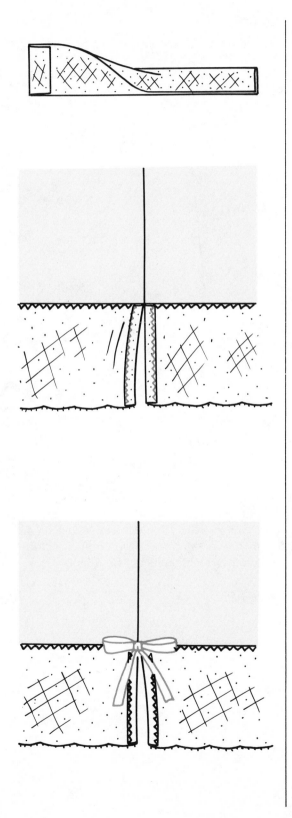

Finish the ends of the lace by using a narrow lace about ½" (1.3 cm) wide with the same design on both sides. Cut two strips as long as the width of the bottom lace plus ½" (1.3 cm). Fold each end under ¼" (6 mm). Then fold the lace lengthwise. Use these pieces as edgings for the bottom lace by inserting the ends of the bottom lace into this edging. Sew this edge on with a zigzag stitch.

For a very "expensive" look, sew a little bow or flower on the top of the slit.

To make this finished look even more "expensive" use a lace for the edging which is a contrasting color with the lace around the bottom of the slip. Make the bow or flower of the same color.

LONG SLIP

Many times you may need a long slip for use under a formal dress. If you do not have a pattern for a long slip, use a pattern for a short slip and extend it by following the outside line on the pattern. The bottom may be finished using any of the methods previously described or you may want a slit at the center front.

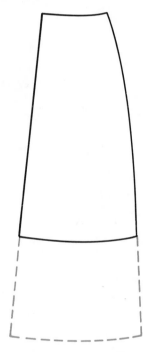

At the bottom of the center front, make a mark 2½" (6.5 cm) and using a 45 degree angle. From the bottom, straight up, make a mark 10½" (27 cm). Make a third mark 6" (15 cm) in from the center front on the hemline. Connect the three marks with a smooth curved line.

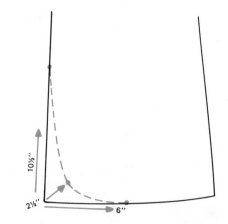

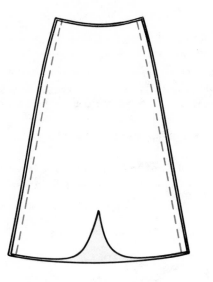

Sew the side seams. At the bottom edge of the slip and at the slit opening on the front, fold the edges under ¼" (6 mm) and topstitch the hem in place. Use either a straight stitch, a small zigzag stitch or you can use a blind hem stitch to make a shell edge. When sewing with a blind hem stitch, the garment should be on the right side of the needle. Be sure that the needle stitches off the fabric when the zig-zag stitch is made.

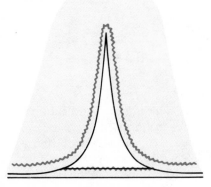

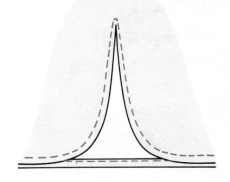

Make a bow from self-fabric, ribbon or use a purchased bow and attach the bow to the top edge of the slit with a few stitches by hand.

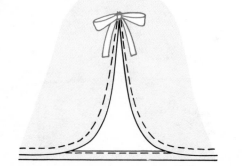

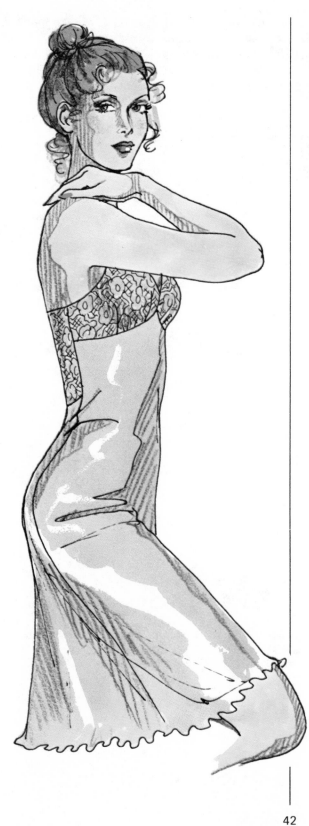

LADIES' FULL SLIP

A full slip takes a little longer time to construct than a half slip as there is a little more detail around the bust line. The bust cups can be made of plain nylon tricot or you can usually find lace sold by the yard. Make certain the lace is wide enough to cover the pattern pieces. If you use lace, remember that it is more comfortable and sturdier to line the cups with nylon sheer or nylon tricot.

When you have cut out the pattern pieces, it will be much easier to avoid mixing them if you mark each piece with a small strip of transparent tape.

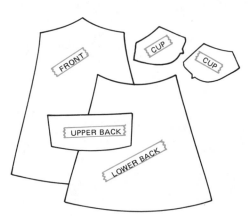

If you plan to use lace and nylon sheer for the bust cup and back yoke, make sure to place the identical lace piece on the sheer piece and to facilitate handling, sew a small zigzag stitch all around the edges. You now have fewer pieces to keep track of. Use a narrow lace to finish the top edge of the slip.

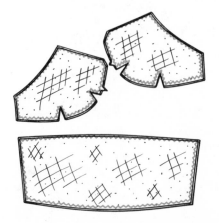

If you plan to use lace around the top edge, we suggest that you sew on the lace before you construct the slip. If the cups are made from lace and sheer, use a narrow lace for the cup edge. If you are making the cups from tricot, you can use lace from narrow up to 2″ (5 cm) wide.

Place the wrong side of the lace on the right side of each cup. Place the center of the design on the lace at the point where the shoulder strap will be placed. The upper edges of the lace should be along the top edges of the cups. At the sides and center front, be sure that the lace is even with the top edge of the cups. Miter the lace at the strap placement point by forming a pleat to fit the shape of the cup.

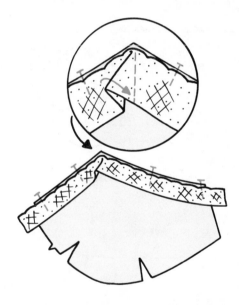

Fold the pleat for the miter to the inside and pin or tape it to hold it in place. Tape or pin the lower edge of the lace to the cup.

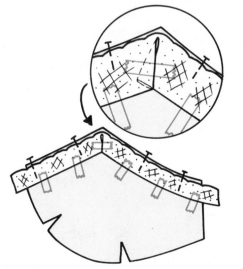

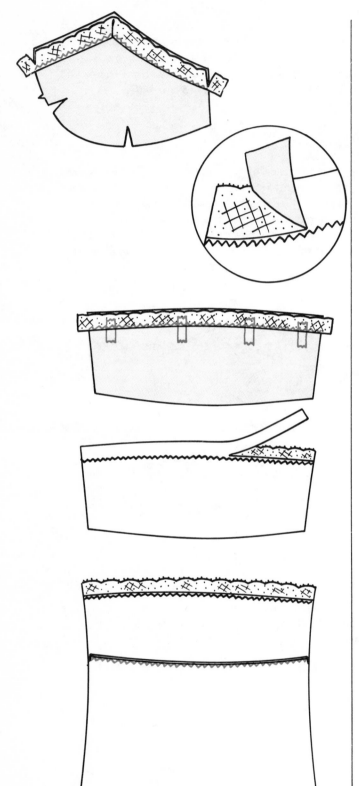

Sew the lace to the cups close to the lower edge of the lace. Trim the lace even with the edge of the cups at the sides and at the center front. Trim the fabric under the lace close to the stitches on the wrong side. On the right side, sew the miter along the folded edge of the lace through all thicknesses of the lace. On the wrong side, trim the excess lace close to the stitches.

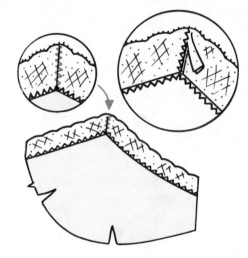

On the back, pin the wrong side of the lace to the right side of the upper back. Place the edge of the lace along the top edge of the back. At the side seams, be sure that the upper edge of the lace is even with the top edge of the back. Pin or tape in place and sew the lace to the back along the lower edge of the lace. Trim the lace even with the side edges of the back. On the wrong side, trim the fabric under the lace, close to the stitches.

With the right sides together, match the center back and side edges and sew the upper back to the lower back.

Sew the cut out darts in each cup, right sides together, using a 1/8″ (3 mm) seam allowance. Sew the cups, right sides together, at the center front seam.

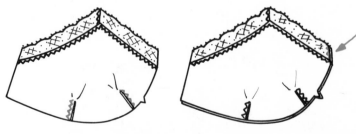

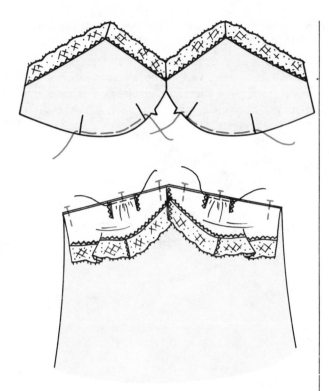

Sew gathering stitches on the bottom edge of each cup between the darts ¼'' (6 mm) from the edges. Pin the front to the cups, matching the center front, notches and side edges. Gather the cups to fit the front. Sew from one side to the center front, lower the needle, turn the fabric and sew to the other side, using a ¼'' (6 mm) seam allowance.

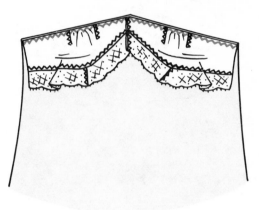

Sew one side seam. Finish the bottom edge of the slip using any of the methods described for a half slip. Sew the other side seam.

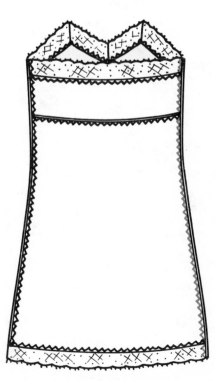

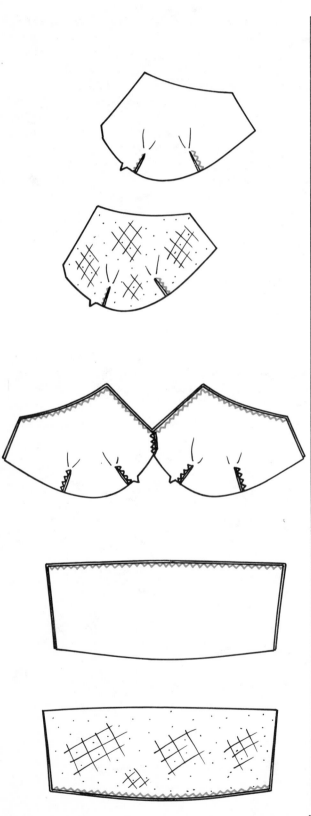

Cups from lace and sheer without narrow lace at top edges.

If you are making the cups from lace and sheer and you do not wish to finish the top edge with a narrow lace, use the following method. Sew the darts for the cups of sheer and lace separately. Sew the center front seams for the cups of sheer and lace separately.

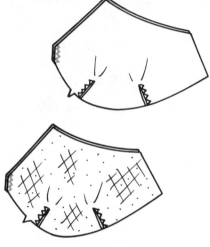

Place the sheer cups on the lace cups, right side to right side, and sew the top edge. Turn the cups right side out. Sew the lace cups to the sheer cups at the bottom edge to keep them together.

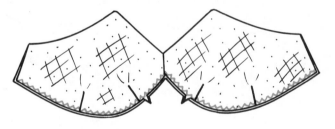

The same method can be used to finish the upper back of the slip. Place the sheer and the lace, right sides together and sew the top edge. Turn right side out and sew the bottom edge together.

Finish the slip as previously described.

For shoulder straps, use either ready-made straps or make a strap. You can make various style straps for a slip; however, most of the better fabric stores which handle lingerie fabric carry a selection of ready-made adjustable slip shoulder straps. These are very inexpensive and will save you a lot of time. If you cannot locate adjustable straps you can usually find ½" (1.3 cm) band which is sold by the yard and can be used for shoulder straps.

If you cannot locate the exact color you need to match the slip it is possible to make the straps yourself using the following procedure:

Cut a 36" (90 cm) length of tricot along the grain 1" (2.5 cm) wide. Fold band double lengthwise, right sides together. Sew a seam as close to fold as you want finished strap to be.

For a flat strap, trim excess tricot close to stitches; for a spaghetti strap which usually is round, leave the seam allowance which will round out the strap. Turn strap to right side.

There are various ways for turning a strap right side out. The easiest way is to cut a little hole in the fold ½'' (1.3 cm) from the edge.

Insert a bobby pin with smooth tips into the opening (hooked through the cup opening) guide bobby pin to other end.

Another method of turning this narrow strap is to place a piece of string inside the strip before you sew it. Sew one end of the string to the fabric. Sew the seam with the string inside.

Now pull on the string and you will turn the strap right side out. Cut this strap in half and use them for the shoulder straps.

For a more interesting effect, if you have used lace on the cups, you can use lace for the shoulder straps. For greater strength, place a ready-made shoulder strap under a narrow lace and sew it on.

48

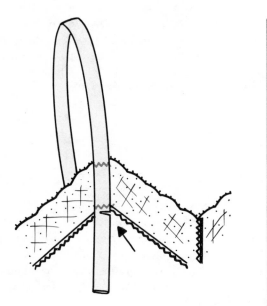

Pin the straps in place on the wrong side but before you sew them on, try on the slip so that you will be certain that the cups are in the correct position.

When you have the shoulder straps in the correct position, sew a seam securely across shoulder strap on right side over seam which attaches the lace to the slip. Trim ends of shoulder straps from wrong side close to stitches.

Another method for attaching the strap when you have a back yoke is to place the right side of the strap on the wrong side of the back at the yoke seam and sew across the strap. Fold up the strap and sew across the strap at the top edge of the yoke.

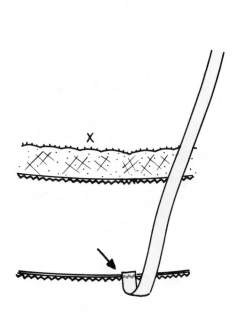

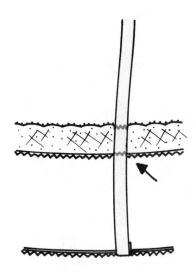

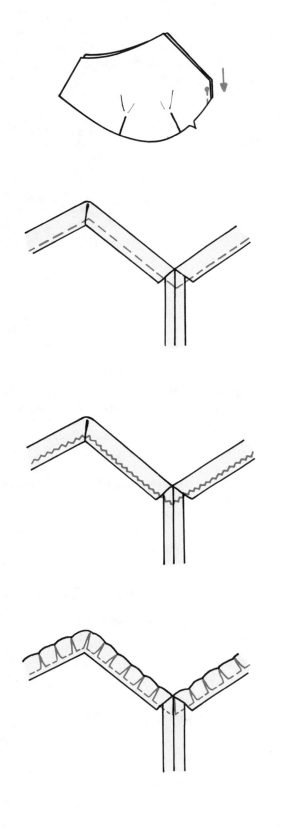

If you do not wish to use lace on the slip, construct the slip as previously described, eliminating the lace. When you are sewing the center front seam of the cups, start sewing ¼" (6 mm) down from the top edge; this will make it easier to turn the top edge for the hem.

The top and the bottom edges of the slip are finished with a narrow hem. Fold a ¼" (6 mm) hem to the wrong side and sew using a straight stitch, small zigzag stitch or you can use a blind hem stitch to make a shell edge. When using a blind hem stitch, the garment should be on the right side of the needle. Be sure the needle stitches off the fabric when the zigzag is made.

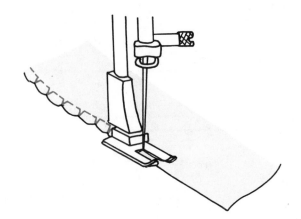

panties

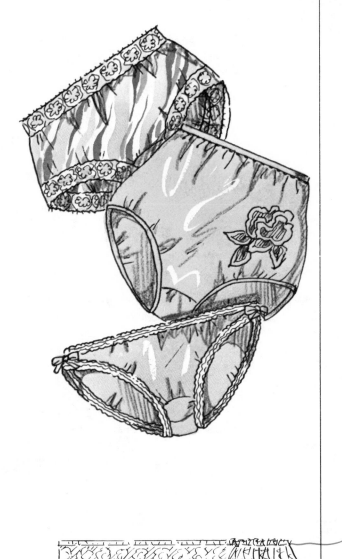

While the saving is not as great when making a pair of panties as it is for other lingerie garments such as a peignoir or nightgown, there is still a considerable saving as you can make as many as four or five pairs of panties from one yard of nylon tricot, which is a very inexpensive fabric. The one exception is panties made with cotton in the crotch area. These are usually very expensive and are required by women who are allergic to nylon in the crotch area. Other women feel that it is more comfortable to have the crotch made from cotton knit.

Panties are available in a great variety of styles. Some are much more expensive than others. Usually pettipants are more expensive so your saving when making this type will be much greater.

Regardless of the style of panties you are going to construct, cut out the pattern pieces remembering that the greatest degree of stretch goes around the body. If you do not remember this, you will not be able to get the panties over your hips. The pattern pieces consist of a front, back and crotch piece. To make it easier for you to line up and sew the crotch, when you cut out the panties, cut a little tab at the center front and center back of the front and back pieces. Cut the crotch piece double; either use two layers of nylon tricot or one layer of nylon tricot and one layer of cotton knit. The stretch in the crotch piece can go either way but you obtain a better fit if the stretch goes across. If you plan to have any type of decoration such as applique or lace, it should be sewn on before you sew the panties together. Always bear in mind that if you use lace for decoration, the lace should go up and down and not crosswise. If you sew the lace on crosswise, it will be difficult to get the panties on. The one exception to this rule is applying lace crosswise to the back of little girls' panties. Gather the lace slightly. This can be done in various ways as follows:

Most lace with a straight edge has a thread going through this edge. Pull this thread slightly and you will gather the lace as much as you wish.

Another method is to sew a gathering stitch on one edge of the lace and then pull the bobbin thread.

Or, instead of gathering the lace, you can stretch the tricot as you sew on the lace. When the tricot returns to its original shape it will gather the lace.

Regardless of the method used to gather the lace, you can sew it on using either a straight stitch or a narrow zigzag stitch. You can either overlap the lace slightly or the strips of lace can be separate.

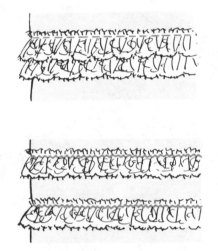

The most common place to use decoration on a pair of panties is on the front. Any decoration should be completed before you sew the panties together. You can use your imagination and place the lace anywhere where you think it will look attractive. You can use a wide lace going from the leg opening to the waist. Or, you may want to use a number of strips of narrow lace in place of the wide lace. These narrow strips of lace should be placed slightly apart. You can also use one wide strip of lace at the center front. You may also place the lace at an angle. Always place the lace on the right side of the fabric, with the wrong side of the lace down.

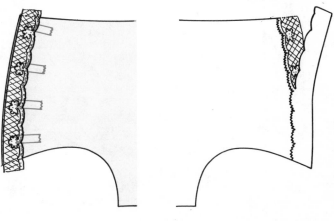

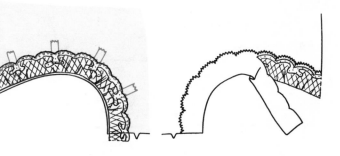

Pin or use tape to hold the lace in place. Sew both edges of the lace using either a straight stitch or a narrow zigzag stitch. Trim the ends of the lace even with the edges of the tricot. You can either leave the tricot under the lace or you can trim away the tricot close to the stitches. Be very careful when you cut the tricot that you do not cut either the lace or the stitches.

Lace around the front legs also adds to the attractiveness of a pair of panties. Place the lace on the front leg opening edge to edge with the bottom edge of the opening. The scalloped edge of the lace should face towards the panties. Sew on the lace on the scalloped edge. Trim the tricot underneath the lace.

Lace can also be placed at the side seam. The straight edge of the lace is placed edge to edge with the side seam. Sew on the lace on the inside edge. Trim off the tricot underneath the lace. If you prefer to have extra strength, do not trim the tricot, both around the front legs and the side seams.

53

Another variation is to place sheer underneath the lace. Sew on through all three layers and then cut away the tricot, leaving the sheer and the lace. On the right side, trim the sheer as close as possible to the stitches.

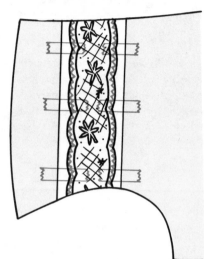 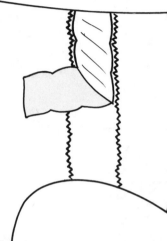 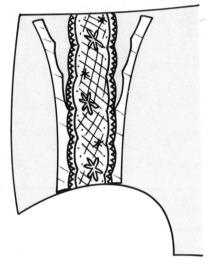

Another variation for trimming the front of panties is to cut a piece of sheer about 2″ (5 cm) wide and long enough to go from the waist to the leg opening. Place the sheer on the front of the panties, right sides up. Place a piece of narrow lace on each side of the sheer. The distance between the lace can vary but a 1″ (2.5 cm) space looks very nice. Tape the lace and the sheer to the panties. Sew along both edges of the lace on both sides. Trim off the tricot on the wrong side under the sheer. Trim the extending edges of the sheer close to the edges of the lace.

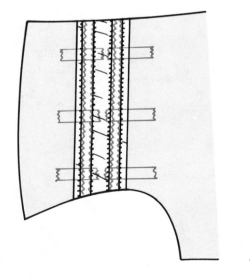 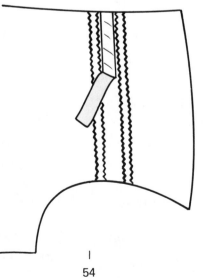 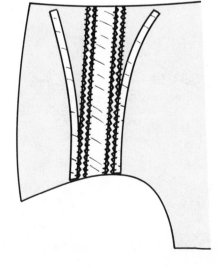

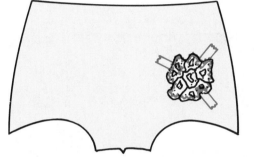

LACE MOTIF

Cut a motif from the lace. Cut along the heavy thread outlining the design. Pin or tape the lace to the front of the panties at one or both sides and sew close to the edge of the lace. On the inside, trim the fabric close to the stitches under the lace. Be careful not to cut the lace.

A variation of applying the lace motif is to use a piece of sheer. The sheer can be the same color as the tricot or it can be a contrasting color.

Place the sheer on the panties with the right side up. Place the flower motif on top of the sheer with the right side up. Sew close to the edges of the lace. Cut the sheer close to the stitches on the right side. On the inside, cut away the tricot under the lace.

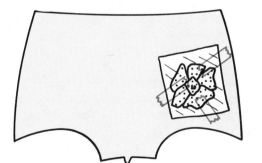

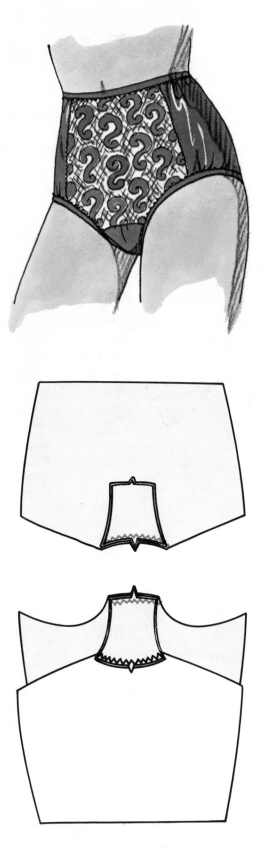

If you would like to have the entire front or part of the front of the panties made of lace, we suggest that you use either tricot or sheer under the lace as lace is not very comfortable when it is next to the skin. If you do use lace on the front, we suggest that you cut the lace on the bias.

If you use lace for the front, place the lace on top of the tricot or sheer and sew around the edges using a small zigzag stitch.

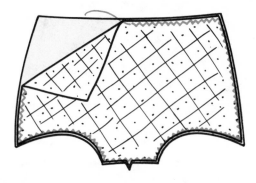

When you have made the decorations on the front of the panties, the construction is the same for regular panties, bikini or children's panties.

The next step is to start sewing the crotch. You can construct the crotch in a couple of different ways but the quickest method, but not the nicest, is to sew a visible crotch seam. Before you sew the side seams, sew the crotch. Place the crotch pieces double, wrong sides together.

Line up the center of the crotch with the center of the back piece. Pin together at this point and at each leg opening. Sew the seam through all three layers. Sew the front crotch seam in the same manner.

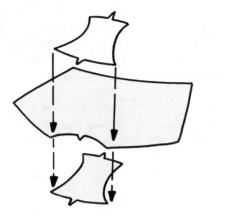

If you prefer a crotch with an invisible seam, place crotch pieces right sides together. Place back piece between crotch pieces, lining up back crotch seam.

Place one pin at center where you have the tab and at both ends of crotch seam. Sew the crotch seam with narrow zig-zag or straight stitch through all three layers.

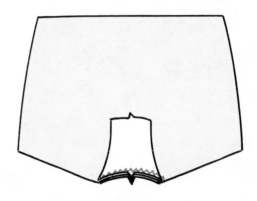

Place front and back pieces right sides together.

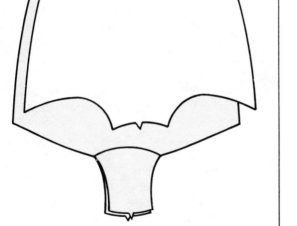

Pin top crotch piece to front, right sides together, matching the tabs.

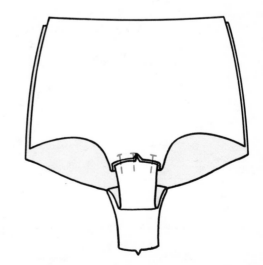

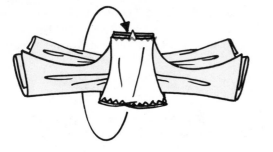

Now wrap bottom crotch piece completely around panties and pin (matching crotch tabs) to front piece, right side of crotch to wrong side of front piece. Front and back of panties are now inside the crotch pieces.

Place pins at center crotch tab and at each leg opening and sew the seam through all layers. Turn panties back into position.

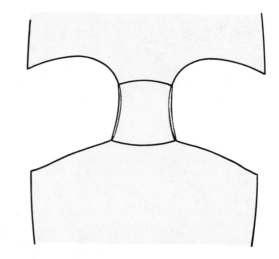

There are various ways to sew the elastic around the leg and the waist opening. These methods are described under elastic in Section 1. Here we will only explain one method for sewing on regular elastic.

As not everyone prefers the same tightness around the legs and the waist, you should always stretch the elastic around the part of the body where it will be worn and determine how much pressure you desire. A general rule to follow is to deduct 2-4" (5-10 cm) from your waist and leg measurement when you cut the elastic.

You can sew on the leg elastic either before or after you have sewn the side seams. We will explain both ways.

Cut two lengths of elastic for the leg openings. We recommend using a ¼" (6 mm) wide elastic. Divide the elastic and the leg opening in fourths with pins.

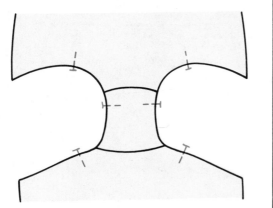

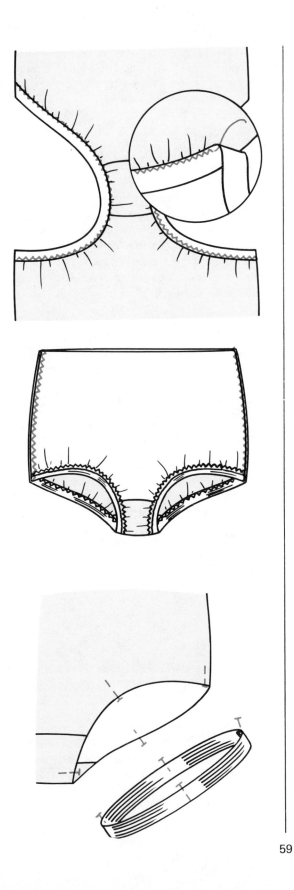

Pin the wrong side of the elastic to the right side of the leg opening, placing the edge of the elastic to the edge of the fabric. Sew close to the inner edge of the elastic, stretching the elastic to fit the opening. Trim the fabric under the elastic, close to the stitches on the wrong side.

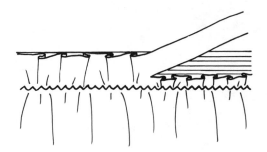

Place the back and the front, right sides together, and sew the side seams.

If you prefer to sew on the elastic after you have sewn the side seams, sew the ends of the elastic together to form two circles. Divide the elastic and the leg openings into fourths with pins. Place the elastic on the right side of the opening, matching the pins. Sew on the elastic, stretching the elastic between the pins to fit the leg opening.

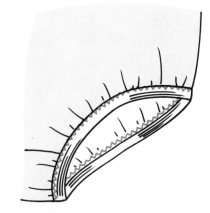

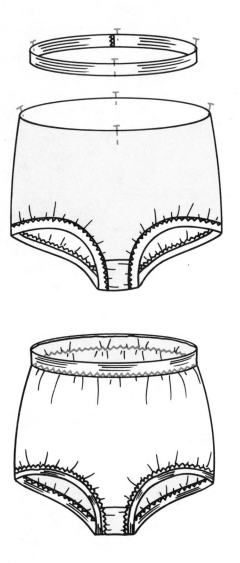

For the waistband, cut one length. We recommend using ½" (1.3 cm) elastic. Sew the elastic into a circle. Divide the elastic and the waist opening in fourths with pins.

Pin the wrong side of the elastic to the wrong side of the opening, matching the pins, with the seam on the elastic at the side seam. The edges of the elastic should be even with the top edge of the panties. Sew on the elastic by sewing on the bottom edge of the elastic, stretching the elastic to fit the fabric. Trim the fabric under the elastic close to the stitches. Turn the elastic to the outside of the panties. Sew a second seam on the other edge of the elastic, stretching the elastic to fit the fabric.

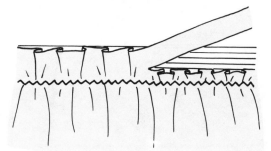

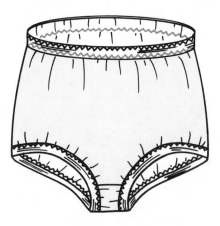

Instead of regular elastic for the panties, you can use stretch lace for both the leg opening and the waist. Use approximately 1" (2.5 cm) wide for the waist and 5/8" (1.5 cm) for the legs.

Sew the elastic into three circles; divide each circle into fourths with pins. Divide the waist and the leg openings into fourths with pins.

Overlap the lace elastic on the right side ½" (1.3 cm); sew the inside edge of the elastic lace, stretching the elastic between the pins. Cut off the excess tricot as close as possible to the stitches from the wrong side.

This is the fastest way to make panties. You only have to sew one seam and you obtain a beautiful finish. Always remember that regardless of whether you use regular lingerie elastic or stretch lace elastic, the seam where the elastic circle is joined should always be on the outside of the leg - not on the inside as it is uncomfortable.

Another method to finish child's panties is to place the lace around the top of the panties underneath the elastic with the lace protruding from under the elastic.

To obtain a very interesting finish, use a wide lace that has the same design on each side.

Fold the lace on a line which is approximately one-third of the lace.

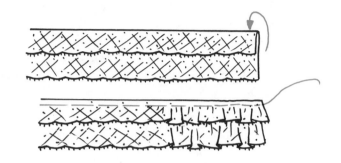

Gather the lace along the fold and then sew the folded edge under the elastic with the wide part of the lace towards the tricot.

You can also use this folded lace for the hem of a night-gown or slip, but in that case you do not gather the lace.

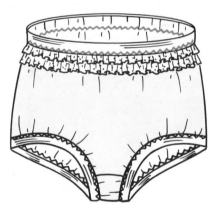

PETTIPANTS

As pettipants are really two garments in one, that is, they are a combination pantie and slip, you should make the pettipants 2'' (5 cm) larger than your hip measurement.

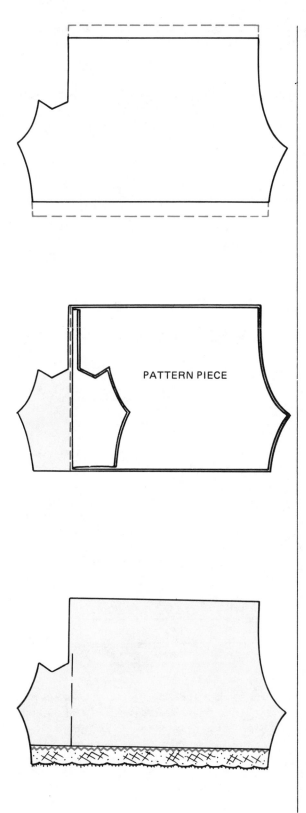

Before you cut the fabric, determine the correct length.

Shorten or lengthen the pettipants at the bottom. If the crotch is too long or too short, lengthen or shorten the crotch area at the waist.

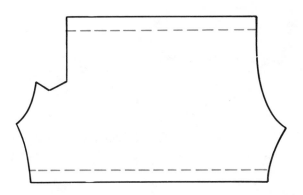

This pattern consists of only one piece so cut it double, right side to right side. Mark the folding pleat line at the front. An easy way to do this is to fold the pattern piece on the pleat line, fold one layer of the fabric over the pattern piece and mark the edge of the fabric where it is folded, mark the bottom layer at the same time using the fold as the guideline. Do not use a pen as it will not wash out. Use a pencil or chalk.

If you are constructing panties with flared legs, pettipants, or any other type of pantie with loose legs and you would like to finish the bottom of the legs with lace, sew the lace on before you sew the panties together. Sew on the lace using the same method as described for the bottom of the half slip. You can either cut away the tricot underneath the lace or you can leave it. Regardless of the method used, always cut away the ends of the lace exactly even with the edge of the tricot. Be sure that you use the same seam allowance all around both leg openings so that the lace matches exactly at the seam.

PATTERN PIECE

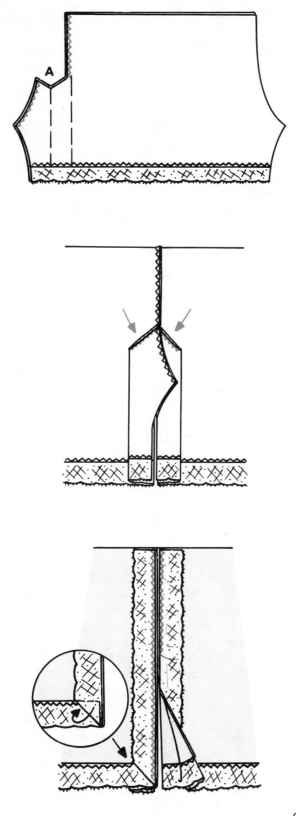

Sew the center crotch seam and the center front. Do not sew the angles at point "A". These are the angles between the crotch seam and the front seam. This is the pleat.

Fold the fabric on the pleat line, wrong side to wrong side. Pin the pleat. Line up the pleat line so that the center front and the pleat line are one straight line.

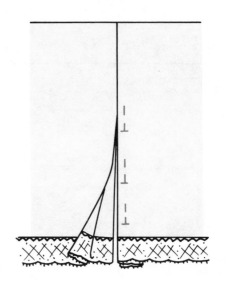

Line up the crotch seam with the center front seam and pin the pleat in place. Sew the pleat in place on the wrong side at the raw edges through the three thicknesses.

Cut two strips of lace the length of the panties from the waist to the leg. Place the straight edge of the lace at the center front seam and the pleat fold. Be sure that the design of the lace matches on both sides of the fold.

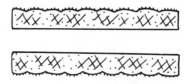

Pin the lace in place through the two thicknesses of the nylon tricot at the pleat. Pin the outer edge of the lace to only one layer of the nylon tricot. Be sure not to catch the pleat. Miter the lace at the bottom of the legs. Stitch the lace on the pleated fold, through two thicknesses and up the center front.

64

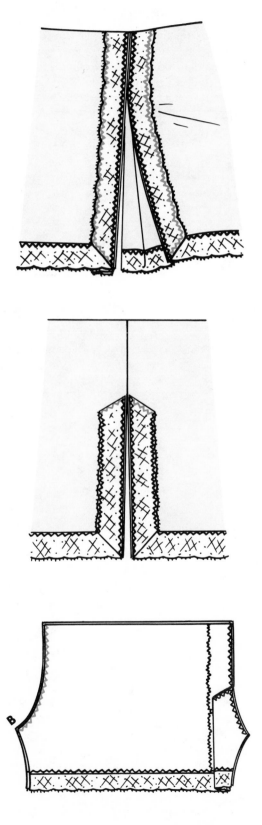

Be sure when you sew on the outside of the lace that you follow the outline of the design on the lace and that you only sew through one layer of nylon tricot. The angle where you mitered the lace at the bottom should only be sewn through the lace.

If you do not wish the lace to go all the way up in front you can arrange the lace around the pleat.

Miter the lace at the top of the pleat and at the bottom of the legs.

Sew the center back seam, making sure that you stop at point "B".
Line up the center front seam with the center back seam and line up the bottom of the legs. Sew the inside leg seams. Use any method you wish to attach the elastic to the top. See Section 1.

65

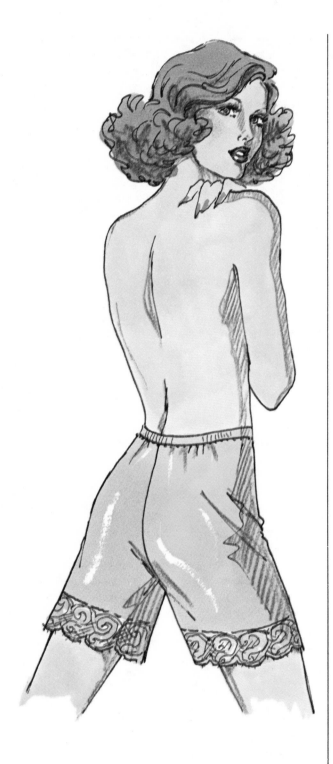

If you prefer a pettipant without a pleat in the front, you can easily adjust the same pattern by folding the pleat on the pattern and line up the center front and the crotch seam before cutting out the pattern.

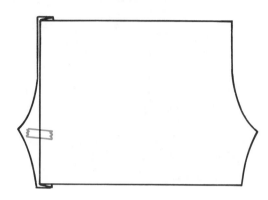

The bottom of the leg can either be trimmed with lace or hemmed.

Sew the panties together by first sewing the center back seam, then the center front seam.

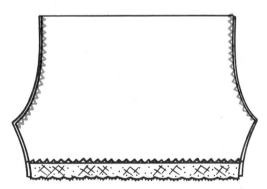

Line up the seams in the same way as for pettipants with pleat and sew up the inside leg seams. Apply the elastic to the waist as described in Section 1.

bras
and
girdles

The idea of making your own bra and girdle has many fascinating aspects. Not only can you create a complete color coordinated ensemble, but for the first time, you can have a bra and girdle that fits you exactly.

Bras can be made from a variety of fabrics. They can be made with non-stretch cotton, heavy weight nylon tricot, or using a combination of nylon tricot and power net.

As KWIK-SEW patterns for girdles and bras are designed for stretch fabrics, this is the only type of fabric we will consider. To be really correct, when working with stretch fabric, you should have a different pattern for each degree of stretch. This is an impossibility as there are so many fabrics on the market with various degrees of stretch. KWIK-SEW patterns are designed for medium stretch. This means that when using material with a great amount of stretch you should use a smaller pattern. For material with less stretch you should use a larger pattern. This is very important especially when you are constructing a girdle.

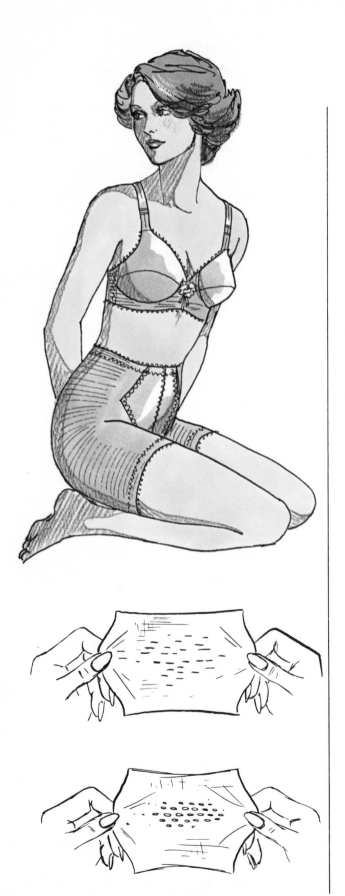

The most important fabric for girdles and bras is power net. For the bra, power net is used for the back piece and under the cups in the front. For a girdle usually the entire girdle is made with power net except for the panels, and even these are often made from power net. This will be discussed in more detail later in this section.

Power net can be found in a variety of weights. These are usually referred to as light, medium and heavy weight. For bras use either light or medium weight; for girdles, we recommend medium weight.

Many women believe that the heavier weight girdle fabric gives a lot more support. While this seems logical, it is not really true as a heavy power net does not return to its original shape as quickly as a lighter weight power net. In addition, it is not as comfortable as a medium weight.

Just as important as using the correct power net is the way the fabric is cut. Usually power net stretches almost the same degree in both directions. It is difficult to determine the greatest degree of stretch which should go around the body.

If you stretch a piece of power net, you can see the holes close. This is the direction of the fabric going around the body.

If the holes are open, this is the straight grain direction.

If you should cut the fabric in the wrong direction, the girdle will still be usable, but it will not last nearly as long as stretching in this direction weakens the fabric.

You can find power net in almost every color, making it possible for you to have a bra and a slip in the same color as your girdle. Rather than picking one of the "run-of-the-mill" colors, this is a wonderful opportunity for you to pick a really exciting color. How about an ensemble in soft green? A flaming red? All black is always useful - especially for darker winter dresses.

Even the elastic which you use for bras and girdles can be obtained in coordinated colors. For a bra you need elastic on both the bottom and the top in order to keep the bra in place.

We recommend using girdle elastic. You can easily tell the difference between girdle elastic and regular lingerie elastic as girdle elastic has one side with a velvety texture which always goes next to the body, regardless if you are making a girdle or bra.

You can find this type of elastic in various widths, starting at around 3/8" (1 cm) wide. For the waist of the girdle, you can use any width elastic between ½" (1.3 cm) and 1" (2.5 cm).

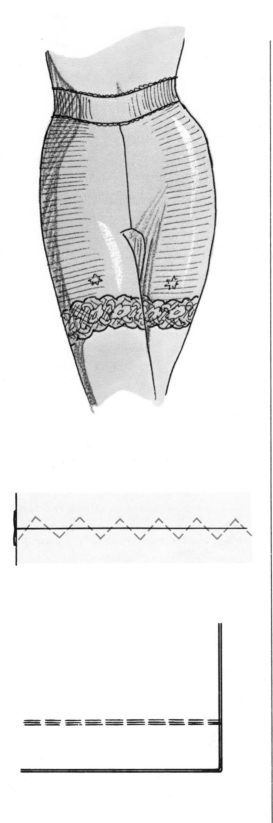

If you want to use a very wide elastic for the waist opening, the elastic will extend above your waistline. A wide type of elastic is usually used around the legs. You can also use stretch lace around the legs, any width can be used.

Regardless of the type of garment you are constructing, every sewing machine has a tendency to skip stitches when you are sewing power net and elastic. This can be corrected by using one or all of the following procedures.

Change the needle to be sure your needle is not dull or slightly bent. Use a fine needle; tighten the pressure on the presser foot and tighten the top thread tension on the sewing machine. As this material has a great amount of stretch, in order to avoid breaking the seam when the fabric is stretched, sew the seams with a narrow zigzag stitch. Even with a zigzag stitch, you have to stretch the fabric while sewing to eliminate the possibility of the seam breaking when the fabric is stretched.

After you have sewn the seam, open the seam allowance. Sew over the opened seam using a large zigzag stitch. Be sure to again stretch the fabric while sewing.

The best stitch to use is an elastic straight stitch which stretches with the fabric. After the seam is sewn, open the seam allowance. Sew over the opened seam using a three-step zigzag stitch.

We do not recommend using a plain straight stitch when constructing a bra or girdle. However, if you want to try sewing the seams with a straight stitch, be sure to stretch the fabric as much as possible as you sew, both in front and in back of the presser foot. Reinforce each seam by sewing two or three rows close together.

BRA

How many times have you tried on a dress only to find that the bra showed a little in the front or perhaps the front view was perfect but a shoulder strap showed.

Now this can be completely eliminated. By constructing your own bra, you can make it of any special design to fit any dress. Low in front; straps far apart; or close together - these variations no longer present a problem.

Not only can you have the correct supporting bra, but you will now be in a position to obtain the perfect line for your garments. Perhaps you would like to give the illusion of a more mature bustline. This is easily done.

KWIK-SEW patterns come in various sizes. Each pattern varies in the cup itself which will result in a perfect fit. Most patterns come in A, B, C and D cups. The size of the cup is determined by the size of the breast.

To choose the correct size pattern, start by measuring under the bust and add 4″ (10 cm) to this measurement. This is the size of the pattern you need.

To determine the cup size, measure around the fullest part of the bust. Now, measure around the body above the bust. Subtract this measurement from the full bust measurement. Every full 1″ (2.5 cm) difference is one cup size. For example, if the difference is 1″ (2.5 cm), choose a cup A. If the difference is 2″ (5 cm), choose a cup B. 3″ (7.5 cm), cup C, etc. In other words, a woman might have a size 34 chest and still have a size A, B or C cup.

As we all know, the distance between the breasts varies from person to person. Some may have them close together - others rather far apart. This distance between the bra cups can easily be altered by adding or subtracting from the center front piece of the pattern.

A bra pattern consists of four pieces. They are back, front, lower cup and upper cup.

You cut two of each piece so that you end with eight pieces of fabric. The back should be made from medium weight power net. The front piece can either be made from medium weight power net or you can use lace plus nylon sheer. The upper and lower cup, the most attractive part of a bra, can be made from nylon tricot which gives the natural look. You can make the cup using only plain lace. If you decide to use lace for the cup, we suggest that you line it with nylon sheer as most lace does not feel comfortable next to your skin, and the sheer will add strength. Cups can also be made from lace covered polyester fiberfill.

To obtain more support on the lower cup, you can add more layers of nylon tricot. If you wish this, then cut two or three pieces of this pattern piece for each cup, or you can use fiberfill for this piece instead of nylon tricot. If you would like to build up the entire bustline to obtain a more mature look, you can make both the lower and upper cup from fiberfill.

When you cut out the patterns, make sure that you follow the arrows on the pattern pieces so that the grain and the stretch of the fabric goes in the correct direction.

If you plan to use more than one layer of fabric on any part of the bra such as lace over sheer for the cups, to facilitate handling, place each lace piece over its identical sheer piece and sew around the edges.

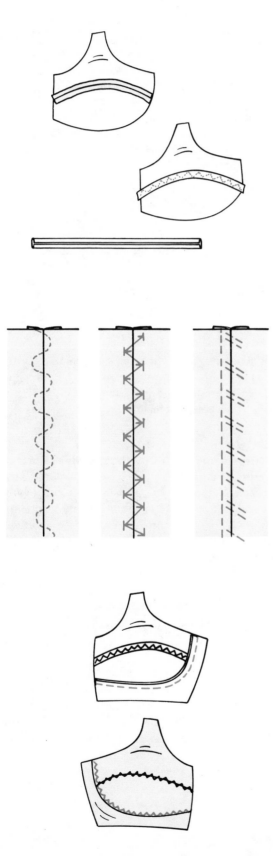

As a bra has so many small pieces, this is a wonderful opportunity to make use of transparent tape. Place a small piece of tape on the pattern pieces and write on the tape what each piece is to be used for.

The easiest method for constructing a bra is to first sew the upper part of each cup to the lower part of the bra cup.

In order to obtain a more professional looking seam, topstitch on the right side over the seam with the seam allowance open. If you prefer, this seam can be covered with bias tape or with a strip of either tricot or sheer. If you are using bias tape, place the tape over the opened seam and sew close to both edges of the tape.

You can topstitch with a wide zigzag stitch or if you have a sewing machine that has a three-step zigzag stitch, you can use this stitch. This stitch has three small stitches within each zig and within each zag. This stitch makes the seam lie flatter.

The topstitching adds strength as well as a more finished look. If you have a reverse cycle sewing machine, you can use one of these decorative stitches for topstitching.

If you wish you may use contrasting thread to give an extra touch to the garment.

Now, sew the seam underneath the cup to the front piece beginning at the side seam. Topstitch with the seam allowance towards the cup.

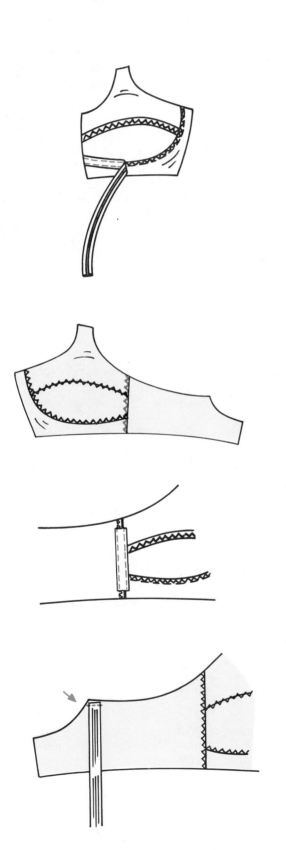

Or, if you prefer to use support wires under the cup, take a piece of narrow bias tape. Place this bias tape on the wrong side of the bra over the sewn seam. Sew the bias tape on using a plain straight stitch as close as possible to the edges of the tape. Sew another seam, up from the bottom edge of the tape so that the wire will stay in place and will not move. Leave enough space so that the wire can be inserted.

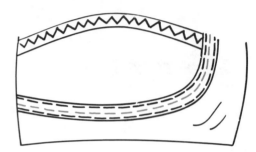

Do not put in the wires until you have completed more sewing as the addition of the wire makes the bra hard to handle. Even if you do not plan to use wire supports, the bias tape will give you a degree of support.

Sew the side seam of the bra. Topstitch with the seam allowance towards the cup. If you prefer, you can put in a stay, using the same method as you used for the support wire. Just remember that the stay has to be slightly smaller than the width of the bra. This also applies to the support wire. The reason for this is that you have to allow a seam allowance for the elastic on the top and bottom of the bra.

The next step is to sew the shoulder straps to the back pieces, as you are still working with two halves - the left and right half of the bra. The best shoulder straps are made with elastic and are adjustable. These can be obtained in many stores. If you cannot locate these straps, they are easy to make. You can purchase regular strap elastic which has a decorative finish on both sides. It is usually 5/8'' (1.5 cm) wide and can be obtained where you purchase your lingerie fabric. Place shoulder strap on right side of back piece, placing the edge of the elastic ¼'' (6 mm) from the edge. See illustration. Sew across the strap using ¼'' (6 mm) seam allowance. Repeat for other strap.

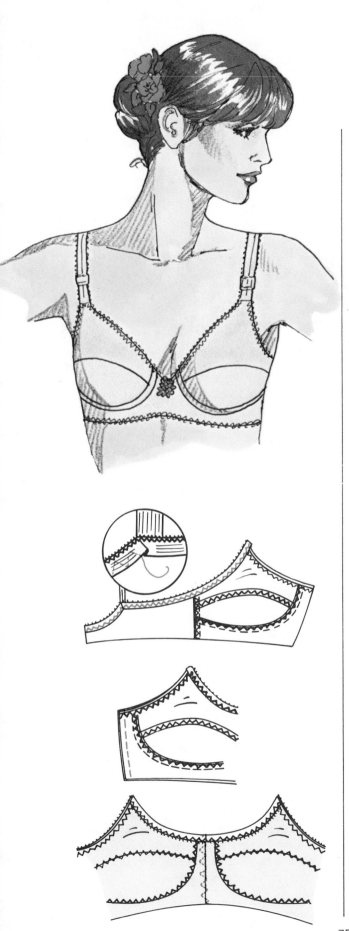

For the top and bottom edges of the bra, use 3/8'' (1 cm) plush elastic. If you prefer, a wide plush elastic can be used at the bottom edge of the bra.

Cut strips of elastic exactly the same size as the pattern pieces as you do not have to make the elastic smaller in this type of garment. Cut one strip for the bottom edge of the bra, two strips for the top edge and two strips for the front V.

If you plan to use support wires, insert these wires before sewing on the elastic. Place elastic plush side up on right side of top edges and front "V's" with the edge of the elastic even with the edge of the fabric. As this type of elastic usually has one ruffled edge, place the ruffled edge so that it is facing down. Sew a seam close to the ruffled edge. We recommend using a narrow zigzag stitch. Trim the fabric under the elastic close to the stitches on the wrong side.

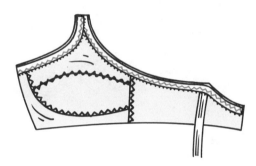

Now turn the elastic to the wrong side and sew a seam on the opposite edge of the elastic using a narrow zigzag stitch or topstitch using a three-step zigzag stitch. Finish only the top edge of the bra from the center back to the shoulder strap placement.

Now pin the left and right bra cup together at the center front. Try on the bra so that you will be sure the cups are in the correct position and not too close or too far apart.

Sew the center front seam; open the seam allowance and topstitch from the right side.

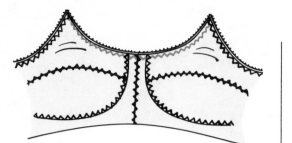

Turn the elastic to the wrong side at top edge of bra and sew a seam on the opposite edge of the elastic.

Sew the elastic on the bottom edge, using the same procedure as on top edge.

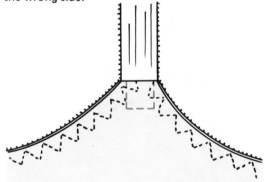

Try on the bra and mark the correct length of the shoulder strap.

Place the shoulder straps on the right side of the bra so that the straps are even with the edges of the bra. Sew across at this point. Trim off top edge of bra close to stitches. Turn the top of the bra to the wrong side and topstitch across to keep the straps in place. Trim the excess length of strap on the wrong side.

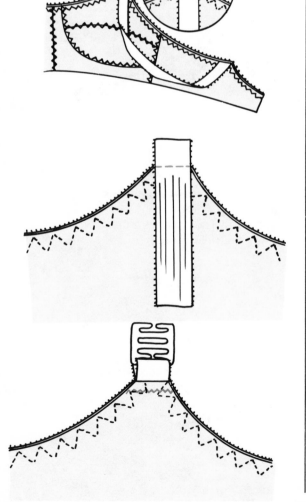

If you wish to have an adjuster so the length of the shoulder strap can be adjusted, cut a piece of strap elastic or 5/8" (1.5 cm) twill tape approximately 2" (5 cm) long. Place this piece on the right side of the bra so that the edges are even. Stitch across at this point. Trim off top edge of bra close to the stitches. Insert an adjuster through the elastic. Fold end of elastic to the wrong side and topstitch across. Cut off excess length of elastic on wrong side.

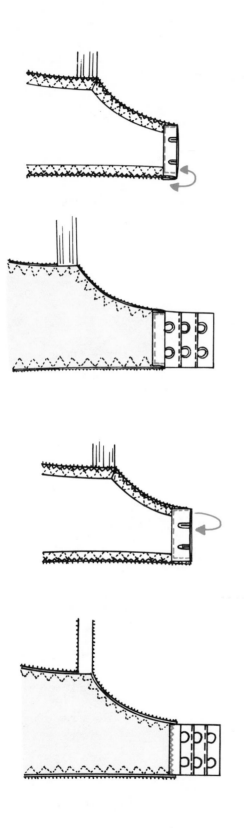

We recommend using a commercial bra fastener at the center back of bra. These are very easy to apply and you obtain a much more professional looking garment. We suggest a fastener 1½" (3.5 cm) wide. Attach the hooks to the right side - the right side is the part of the bra that goes around the right part of your body - and the eyes to the left side.

There are two basic types of hooks and eyes. One type is finished so that you merely insert the ends of the bra in the fastener and topstitch in place. This applies for both the hooks and the eyes. How to attach the unfinished type is described as follows:

HOOK HALF: Place the hook half on the bra, right side to right side, edge to edge. Sew a seam as close as possible to the hooks.

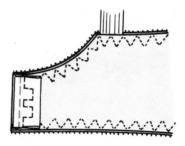

It will be approximately ¼" (6 mm) from the raw edge of the center back. Turn the hooks to the wrong side and topstitch on remaining three edges.

EYE HALF: Overlap the eye half ¼" (6 mm) on the other back edge, placing the wrong side of the eye half on the right side of the fabric. Topstitch securely.

After you have attached the hooks and eyes, trim the sides so that they are the same width as the back of the bra. Overcast the edges with a close zigzag stitch.

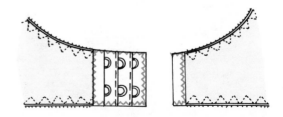

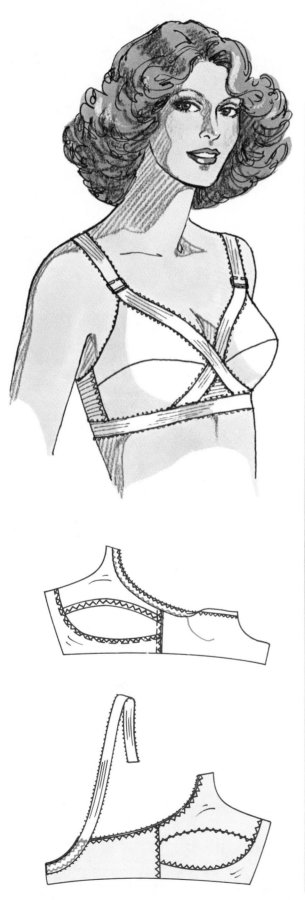

BRA VARIATION: Using the same pattern, you can easily change it so that you have cross elastic in the front. Sew the bra together as previously described up to the point where you apply the elastic.

Apply the elastic to the top edge of the top side of the bra first. Place the elastic, plush side up, on the right side of the top edges of the side of the bra. Place the ruffled edge of the elastic so that it is facing down. Sew a seam close to the ruffled edge. Trim the fabric under the elastic close to the seam.

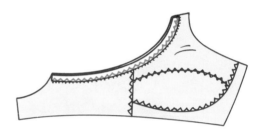

Turn the elastic to the wrong side and sew a seam on the opposite edge of the elastic using a narrow zigzag stitch or topstitch using a three-step zigzag stitch.

Cut two strips of strap elastic long enough for the top edge of the back and the shoulder straps, approximately 22" (56 cm) long. Place the ends of the elastic, edge to edge, with the center back by overlapping the elastic so that it is edge to edge with the top edge of the back. The right side of the elastic should be up. The finished width of the center back has to be the same width as the fasteners. The center back can be decreased or increased. The strap can be sewn closer to the bottom edge, or closer to the top for a wider fastener.

Sew on the elastic on the inner edge. Sew another seam ¼" (6 mm) from the seam. On the wrong side, trim the fabric close to the stitches.

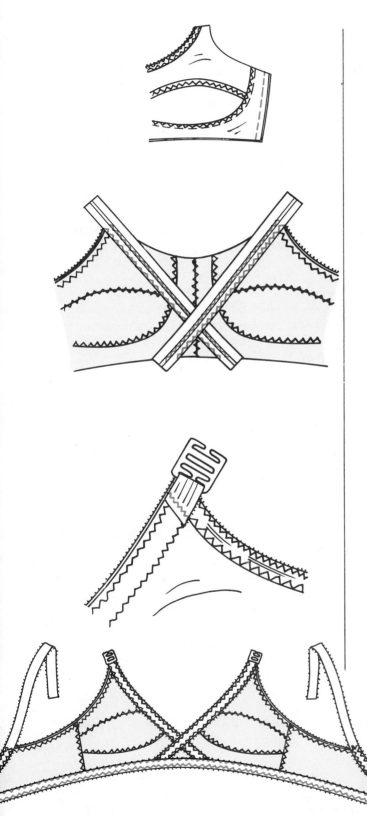

Now sew the center front seam of the bra. Open the seam allowance and topstitch on the right side.

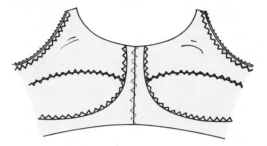

Use strap elastic for the front. Pin the ends of the elastic at the bottom of the front approximately 1¼" (3.2 cm) from the center front. Continue to pin the elastic up to the point where you normally would locate the shoulder straps. Extend the elastic 1" (2.5 cm) up from the strap placement. It is not necessary to follow the edge of the bra. This will give you a deeper V.

Before sewing on the elastic, try on the bra so that you are certain the shoulder straps are in the correct position and that they feel comfortable. Sew on the elastic on the inner edge of the elastic. Sew another seam on the elastic ¼" (6 mm) from the first stitching. On the wrong side, trim the fabric close to the stitches.

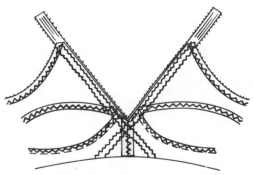

Insert an adjuster through the extending strap elastic. Fold the elastic to the wrong side and sew across.

Now finish the bottom edge of the bra. You can use the same elastic as you used for the straps. Place the elastic, edge to edge, with the bottom edge of the bra. Topstitch close to the bottom edge. Sew a second seam ¼" (6 mm) from the edge. Apply hooks and eyes to back of bra.

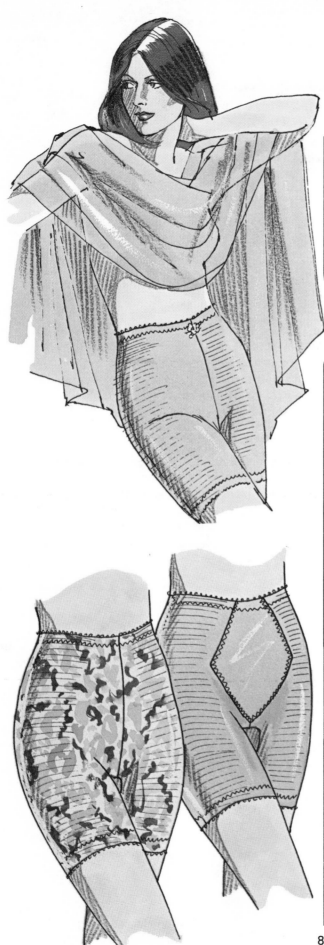

GIRDLES

As you know, there are various types of girdles and all of them are easy to construct. Since they require only a small amount of fabric, the cost will be only a fraction of what you would pay for a ready-made garment. In addition to the savings involved, this is the only time in your life when you will have a girdle with perfect fit. There is no rule as to how tight or loose a gridle should be. This is a matter of personal preference.

KWIK-SEW has girdle patterns designed for Sizes 8 to 22. As you are working with an extremely stretchy fabric, you cannot check your own measurement with the pattern pieces. The pattern pieces are much smaller than your body measurement.

Therefore, it is very important to check your body measurements with the chart found on the back of the pattern envelope. Also check the fabric for the correct stretch on the chart on the back of the envelope or in Section I.

If you wish to have a support panel, it can be placed where-ever you need it. However, it is not necessary to have a support panel. If you do not need one, do not make one.

The best fabric for the panel is a one-way stretch fabric. Here is one case where you do not follow the rule of the stretch going around the body. For the panel, the stretch goes up and down as this gives you more support. You can also use a non-stretch fabric for the panel, but only for the stomach front. This type of fabric would feel very uncomfortable when you sit if it were used for the sides and back.

If you do not require as much extra support, you can use a double layer of two-way stretch power net. In this case, cut the panel with the greatest degree of stretch going up and down.

Regardless of the style of girdle you plan to make, you use the same general technique.

When you topstitch the seams and when you are sewing on the panels, you can topstitch with a wide zigzag stitch or if you have a sewing machine that has a three-step zigzag stitch, you can use this stitch. This stitch has three small stitches within each zig and within each zag. This stitch makes the seam lie flatter. The topstitching adds strength as well as a more finished look. If you have a reverse cycle sewing machine, you can use one of these decorative stitches for topstitching. If you wish, you may use contrasting thread to give an extra touch to the garment.

When you are using a separate crotch piece, it will be more comfortable if you make this piece from one or two layers of nylon tricot rather than power net. The length of the legs can be as long as you wish or you can cut them off completely - in which case you will have a girdle brief. Bear in mind not to make the legs too tight as this will cause the girdle to wrinkle up. Also, if the legs are too tight, the girdle may cut off the blood circulation causing your legs to swell.

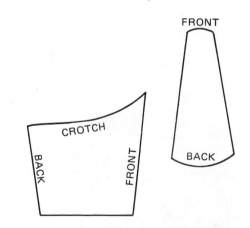

Cut out all the pattern pieces in medium weight power net. Cut the crotch piece in nylon tricot. Mark the back and front of the inside leg pieces and the crotch piece as it is very easy to mix up these pieces.

Sew the center front seam using a ¼" (6 mm) seam allowance. Open the seam allowance and topstitch on the right side.

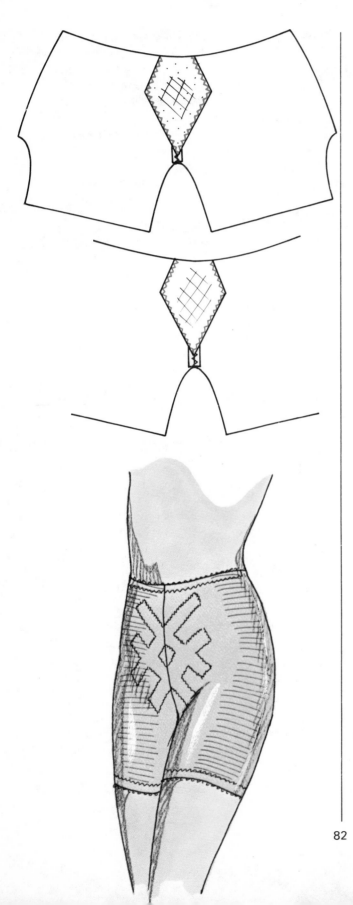

If you plan to use panels, cut out the pieces. Place the girdle flat with the wrong side up. If you are going to use a panel in the front, place the right side of the panel to the wrong side of the girdle. Remember, for the panel, if you are using one-way stretch, the stretch has to go up and down. Pin the panel in place. Sew the panel to the girdle around the edges using any stitch you prefer.

Turn the girdle to right side and trim off the power net ¼'' (6 mm) from the seam. Sew a second seam on this cut edge all around the panel.

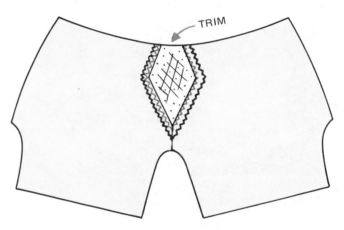

When you are using two-way stretch power net, you can use it for a panel or criss-cross. Cut the power net in the opposite direction than the girdle as this will give you more support. Place this panel on the wrong side of the girdle and sew around the edges.

When using a criss-cross support, sew the strips on the wrong side of the girdle. The number of strips depends upon how much support you need.

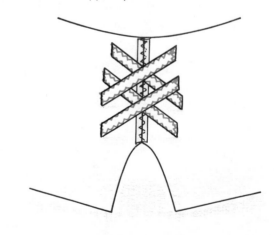

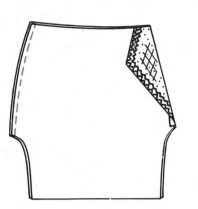

When you use two-way stretch power net for additional support, do not cut away the girdle fabric underneath as you do for one-way stretch panels or non-stretch panels. Here you need the two layers for extra support. Use the above procedures for attaching side panels.

Place the girdle right sides together and sew the center back using ¼" (6 mm) seam allowance. Open the seam allowance and topstitch.

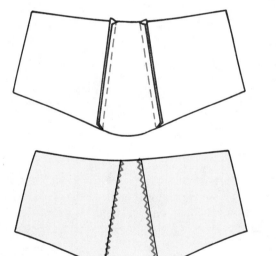

If you decide to have a panel in the back, or if you wish criss-cross supports, do it using the same methods as described for the front.

Now, sew the nylon crotch piece to the inside leg seam right side together using ¼" (6 mm) seam allowance. Topstitch from the right side with the seam allowance towards the inside of the legs.

If you would like to have an invisible crotch seam, cut two crotch pieces of tricot. Place the crotch pieces right sides together, on each side of the leg piece. Sew through all three layers.

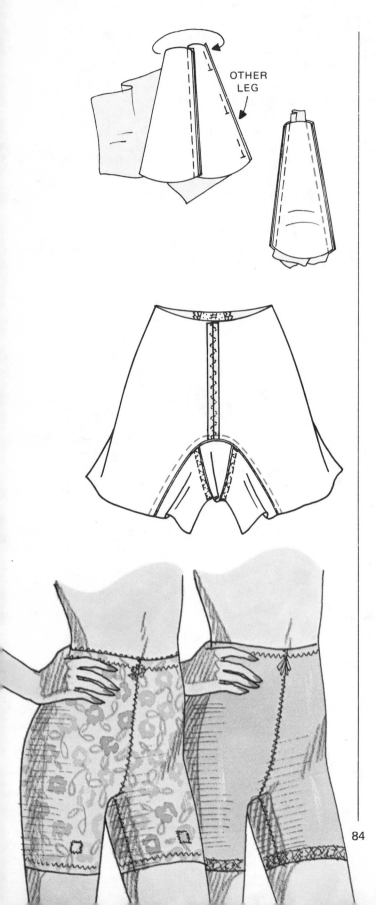

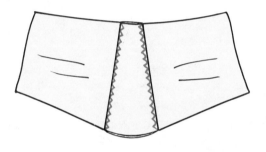

Pin the other leg piece to the top crotch piece, right sides together.

Fold the other crotch piece completely around and pin the right side of the crotch piece to the wrong side of the leg piece. The crotch is now right sides together with the leg pieces in between. Sew through all three layers. Turn the crotch right side out. Topstitch the crotch piece using either a zigzag stitch or a three step zigzag stitch. Sew close to the seam.

Pin center back of crotch to center back seam. Be sure to line up the bottom edges of the legs, right sides together. Sew back leg and crotch seam in one operation.

Topstitch the leg seam with the seam allowance towards the inside of the legs.

Before you decide what type of elastic you would prefer around the leg openings, you should decide if you want to have garters or the new type of rubberized elastic which will hold up your stockings without garters.

If you plan to use elastic lace around the bottom of the legs, any width will do as this is mostly used to give the girdle a more finished appearance. Elastic lace can be obtained in many different designs with various degrees of stretch. The width also varies considerably. Your personal preference will decide which elastic lace you use. It is difficult to see which is the correct side on some types of lace. In this case you can use either side but be sure to use the same side on each leg. Cut two strips of elastic lace exactly the length of the leg openings; attach this elastic lace by overlapping approximately ½'' (1.3 cm) on right side of the legs.

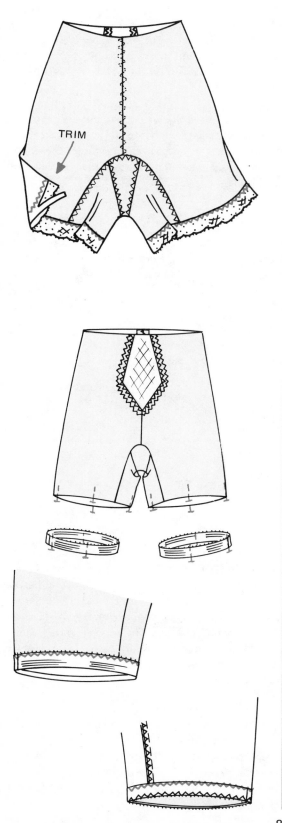

Sew the elastic lace on using a zigzag stitch on the inner edge of the elastic lace. Cut off the excess power net on the wrong side close to the stitches.

Pin the center front of the crotch to the center front seam with the right sides together. Make sure that the lace at the bottom of the legs lines up exactly. Sew the front crotch seams together using ¼'' (6 mm) seam allowance. Top-stitch from the right side with the seam allowance towards the inside of the legs.

If you plan to use regular girdle elastic or the rubberized elastic on the leg openings, sew the front crotch seam before you sew the elastic. Then cut two lengths of elastic or rubberized elastic long enough to go around the leg opening. Sew them together to form two circles.

Overlap the elastic ¼'' (6 mm) on the right side of the leg opening with the velvety side up and with the fancy edge towards the girdle. Sew the elastic on with a zigzag seam close to the fancy edge.

Fold the elastic over to the wrong side and using a zigzag seam, sew on the other edge of the elastic.

Be sure to place the seam on the elastic on the outside of the legs as this seam can be very hard - especially when you are using the rubberized elastic and this will sometimes be very uncomfortable on the inside of the leg.

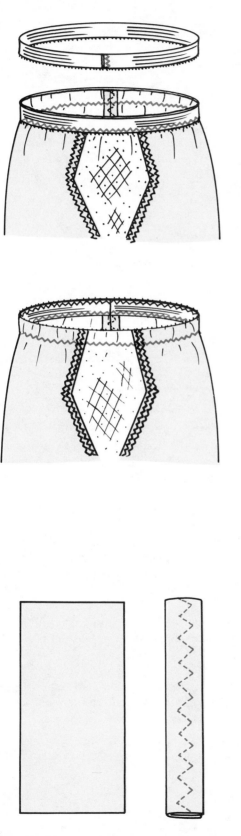

Now try on the girdle and mark the top of the girdle where you want the waistline. Trim off the excess ¼" (6 mm) above where you want the waist to be as this is the seam allowance for the elastic. Cut the waistband elastic the same length as the opening.

If you prefer to have the waist opening very tight, you can cut the elastic smaller. Apply the elastic in the same manner as you used for the bottom of the girdle, but be sure to place the elastic seam in a place where it will not feel uncomfortable.

You can buy small roses or other designs which can be appliqued to the center front of the top of the girdle to give the girdle a touch of beauty.

If you plan to use garters instead of rubberized elastic around the legs, mark on the wrong side of the legs where you want to have the garters. You can use either two or three garters on each leg. If you are using two garters, we suggest that they be placed approximately 2" (5 cm) from the front inside leg seam. The second garter should be placed 2½" (6.5 cm) from the inside leg seam at the back. The garters should be placed approximately 2" (5 cm) up from the bottom edge.

If you cannot buy the garter fastener in the color you wish, you can take regular girdle elastic and use it for the fastener. Or, you can make them from girdle fabric. Cut strips of fabric approximately 4" (10 cm) long and 1½" (4 cm) wide for each garter fastener. Fold over lengthwise so that you get three thicknesses and sew down the middle with a stretchy seam such as a three-step zigzag.

Sew the garters to the wrong side of the girdle with the garters facing down. Cut a small piece of power net or nylon tricot about the size of a quarter. Place this piece on top of the point where you have sewn on the garter. Sew this piece around the edges. Now you will not be annoyed by the garter seam.

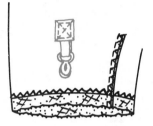

To cover up the garter stitches on the right side, you can either sew a little applique on the right side of the girdle or you can cut out a design from a piece of stretch lace and place it over the stitches. Sew around the edges and this will cover up the stitches.

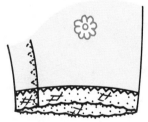

GIRDLE BRIEF: Many women prefer to have a little support and do not wish to use a regular girdle. A girdle brief will take care of this need and it is often used when wearing shorts or slacks.

Cut out the back and the front pattern pieces using two-way medium stretch power net. Cut two crotch pieces using nylon tricot. We recommend using 3/8'' (1 cm) wide girdle elastic for the waist and leg openings. To obtain the correct length, measure the elastic around your waist and around legs so that it feels comfortable.

Sew on the crotch using the same method you use when constructing a pair of panties. Place the back and front, right side to right side, and sew the side seams using a ¼'' (6 mm) seam allowance. Open the seam allowance and top-stitch the seam on the right side using a zigzag stitch or a three-step zigzag stitch.

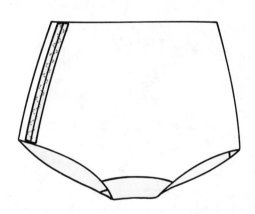

Sew the elastic lengths securely together to form circles; the velvety sides of the elastic should be together. Use a ¼'' (6 mm) seam allowance.

For the waist and leg openings, overlap the elastic circles ¼'' (6 mm) over the right side of the openings, the velvety side up. Place seam on the elastic at center back. For the leg openings, place the seam at the side seams. Sew a seam on the velvety side of the elastic close to the edge. Stretch the elastic and the fabric as you sew the seam. Turn the elastic to the wrong side. Sew a seam on the other edge of the elastic. Stretch both the elastic and the fabric as you sew.

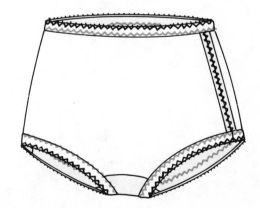

gowns

You can save more money when you sew your own gowns, robes and peignoirs than you can by sewing any other lingerie garment. For some mysterious reason, these garments are often extremely expensive when you shop for ready-made garments. Perhaps it is because they are so often purchased for gifts in the more exclusive type stores. Even in the more exclusive type stores, you often have to look hard before you can find a really luxurious looking garment and even then it is often almost impossible to buy a gown and a robe, or a gown and a peignoir which are perfectly matched. For example, the robe may fit perfectly and have the exact design you are looking for, but the gown may be too tight over the bust.

Equally as important as saving money and obtaining a perfect fit, you can have fun constructing these garments as you can let your imagination run wild with the use of lace, sheer, appliques, trim and colors. Leading fabric stores now carry a great variety of fabrics and notions which are suitable for these garments.

There are many patterns on the market for various styles of robes, gowns and peignoirs. All the various ideas in this section for decoration, finish or finishing touches can be used on almost any pattern.

A master pattern for gowns is included in the back of this book. You can construct six designs using various overlayers. For all the various designs, the pattern is the same from the bottom of the bust down. You use the same pattern for the back and the front skirt. The master pattern comes in sizes small, medium, large and extra large.

It is very important that you choose the correct size. Compare your body measurements with the chart in Section I and determine which is your correct size. Also, remember to check for the correct length.

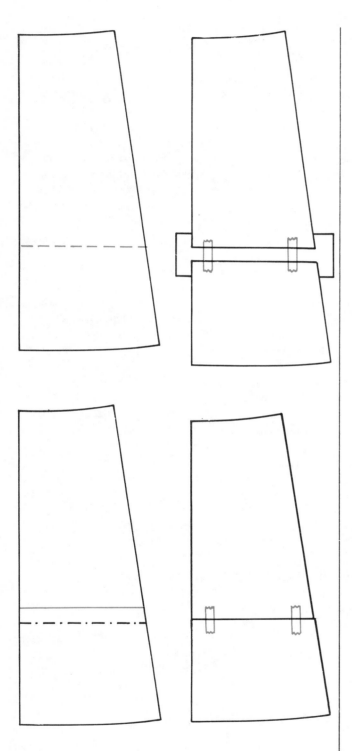

Each size is color-coded so you merely choose the size you desire, follow the colored lines as you trace the pattern. You should not cut out the pattern as the pattern is printed on both sides of the paper. You can use the pattern over and over, making various changes. We suggest using Kwik-Trace which is manufactured using pressed fibers and it has one inch spaced dots which makes it easier for you to make changes on the pattern.

The most common change you have to make is in the length. If you have to shorten or lengthen the pattern, use the line indicated on the pattern for shortening or lengthening. To lengthen the pattern, cut the pattern pieces apart at this line, place a strip of paper underneath the pattern, separate the pattern the amount you need and tape the pieces in place. Draw lines on the sides to restore the pattern to its original shape. Cut off any excess paper.

To shorten the length, either make a fold and tape in place or you can cut the pattern apart and overlap by the correct amount. Restore the side seams to their original shape.

In order to avoid making a mistake when you fold the pattern, from the line, measure up the total amount you wish to shorten the pattern. Make another line at this point. Fold one line up to the other line. If you do not do this, you could easily make a fold which would give you double the amount needed.

The pattern is designed for use with stretch or non-stretch fabric. Because these garments are loosely fitted, you do not have to have a special pattern for woven and a different pattern for knit fabric. Some suggested fabrics are nylon tricot, nylon sheer, brushed nylon, crepeset, single knit or any lightweight cotton or blends.

The sewing procedures will be slightly different when you are using different fabrics. For knit fabrics you can use the ¼" (6 mm) seam allowances which are included in the pattern. If you are using nylon tricot or sheer, the seam allowances can be trimmed to 1/8" (3 mm) at the side and sleeves seams.

If you are using woven fabric, you can use the ¼" (6 mm) seam allowance or you can add to the seam allowances to include a 5/8" (1.5 cm). We prefer to have a ¼" (6 mm) seam allowance on sleepwear even when you are using woven fabric. For sewing seams, see Section I.

You can construct a nightgown using either one or two layers of fabric.

For a two layer nightgown you can use any suitable fabric but if you are using nylon tricot, a top layer of nylon sheer may be used or you may prefer to use two layers of nylon sheer. We do not suggest using two layers of nylon tricot as this would be rather bulky and does not look very attractive. One suggestion, often a much more glamorous look can be obtained if you do not use the same color for each layer. Try to get a printed nylon sheer for the outer layer. Because this material is so thin, you will be amazed to see how the color seems to shine through the sheer, giving you the impression of an entirely different color than is found in each layer of fabric, if you looked at them separately.

If you prefer to have a solid color, it is always safe to use a top layer in beige or white over the nylon tricot. As the beige or white nylon sheer will pick up the color of the tricot underneath, it will give a much more subdued effect.

When you are using two layers of fabric, we suggest that for the skirt part of the gown you make the top layer slightly wider than the bottom layer. At the center front and the center back, increase the width 2" (5 cm). Place the front and the back 2" (5 cm) from the folded edge of the fabric. This will make the gown 4" (10 cm) wider in the front and back.

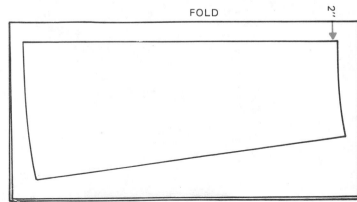

VIEW A

The gown in View A can be made with short, elbow length or long sleeves. This is a very simple gown and is easy to construct. For chilly nights, this gown can be made using flannel; actually, almost any fabric may be used. Trace Pattern Pieces 1, 2, 3 and 4. Decide what length you would like to have for the gown and the sleeves. You have to trace the No. 1 piece twice for the back and the front. Cut out the pattern pieces.

Tape Pattern Piece No. 2 on to the top of Pattern Piece No. 1 on the line marked. This makes the front of the gown. Tape the other No. 1 pattern piece to No. 3 pattern piece. This is the back of the gown. Pattern Piece No. 4 is the sleeve. For this gown, refer to the chart for the amount of fabric which you need.

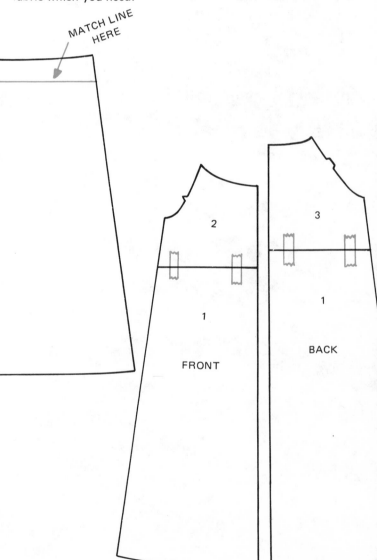

92

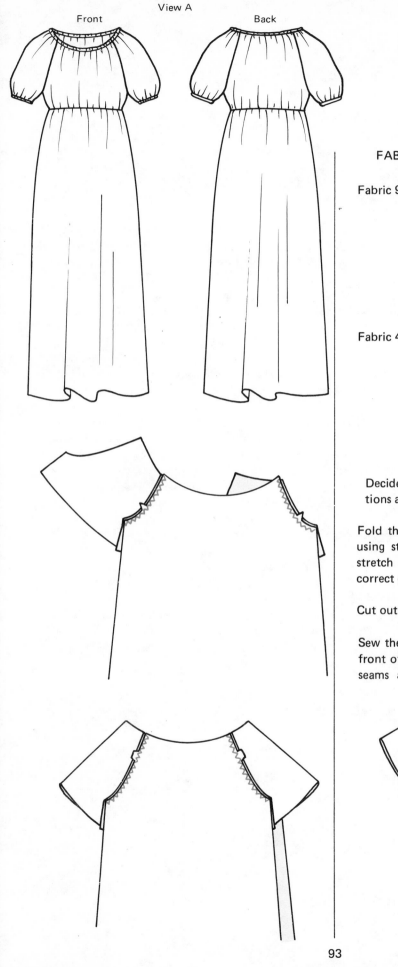

Front   Back

FABRIC REQUIRED FOR SINGLE LAYER GOWN
FOR ALL SIZES

Fabric 96"(249cm) to 108" (274cm) wide

long gown, long sleeves	2 3/8 yd (2.20m)
short gown, long sleeves	1 7/8 yd (1.75m)
long gown, elbow length sleeves	2 1/8 yd (1.95m)
short gown, elbow length sleeves	1 5/8 yd (1.50m)
long gown, short sleeves	2 yd (1.85m)
short gown, short sleeves	1 1/2 yd (1.40m)

Fabric 45"(115cm) wide

long gown, long sleeves	4 1/8 yd (3.80m)
short gown, long sleeves	3 3/8 yd (3.10m)
long gown, elbow length sleeves	3 7/8 yd (3.55m)
short gown, elbow length sleeves	3 1/8 yd (2.85m)
long gown, short sleeves	3 3/4 yd (3.45m)
Short gown, short sleeves	2 7/8 yd (2.65m)

Decide how the gown will be finished and purchase notions accordingly.

Fold the fabric double, right side to right side. If you are using stretch fabric, be sure that the greatest degree of stretch goes around the body and follow the arrows for correct grain.

Cut out the fabric for the gown.

Sew the back of the sleeve to the back of the gown and the front of the sleeve to the front of the gown. Sew the sleeve seams and the side seams in one continuous operation.

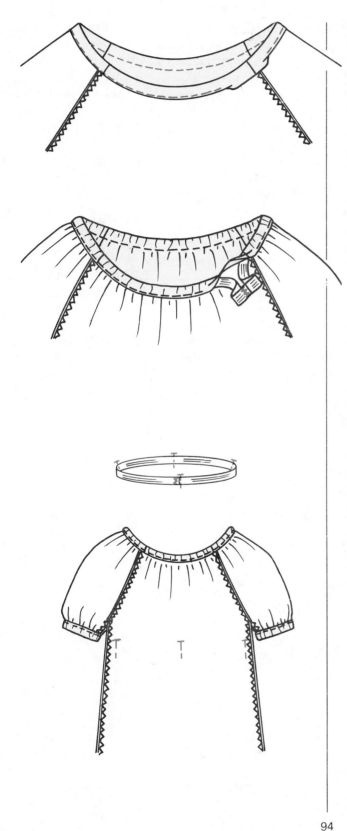

There are various ways to utilize elastic around the neckline, at the bottom of the sleeves and at the bottom of the bustline or around the waist. The easiest method is as follows:

Make the casing for the elastic at the bottom of the sleeves and the neck opening. Turn the edge of the fabric to the wrong side ½" (1.3 cm), turn under the raw edges and sew a seam as close to the edge as possible. Be sure to leave a small opening for inserting the elastic. Cut a length of elastic for the neck opening; for Size Small, use 27½" (70 cm) elastic; for Medium, use 28¼" (71 cm); for Large, use 29" (73 cm); for Extra Large, use 29¾" (75 cm). Cut two lengths of elastic for the sleeve. To determine the length, place the elastic around your arm so that it feels comfortable.

Insert the elastic at the bottom of the sleeves and at the neck opening. Overlap the ends of the elastic and sew them together. Close the opening in the casing where you inserted the elastic.

Try on the gown, decide where you want the elastic, either under your bustline or you may want the elastic at the waistline. Mark the point where you would like to have the elastic, across both the back and the front.

Cut one strip of ¼" (6 mm) elastic. To obtain the correct length, measure the elastic around that part of the body where it will be used so that it feels comfortable. Sew the ends of the elastic to form a circle. Divide the circle in fourths with pins. Where the elastic goes, divide the garment in fourths with pins. Place the elastic on the wrong side of the gown, matching the pins. As you sew on the elastic, stretch the elastic to fit the fabric. Sew a seam on top of the elastic; we recommend using a large zigzag stitch or a three step zigzag stitch.

If you would like to have the elastic adjustable around the neck and under the bust by using a tie, use the following procedure.

For the neck opening, mark the center front of the neck opening. Make a buttonhole on each side of the mark ½" (1.3 cm) apart and 5/8" (1.5 cm) down from the raw edge.

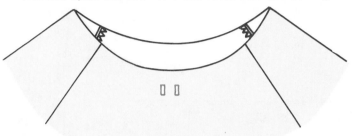

Make the casing as previously described. Cut one strip of elastic 20" (51 cm) long. Make two ties by cutting two strips of fabric 15" (38 cm) long and 3/4" (2 cm) wide. Fold each strip double lengthwise, right side to right side. Sew a seam the length of the tie. Turn the tie right side out. See Section II for slips for an easy method to turn the tie. Insert the elastic into the ends of the tie and sew securely across at both ends of the elastic.

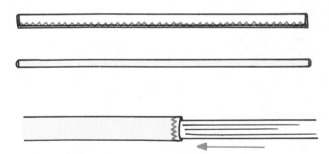

Insert the elastic in the casing through the buttonhole. Make a small knot at the end of each tie.

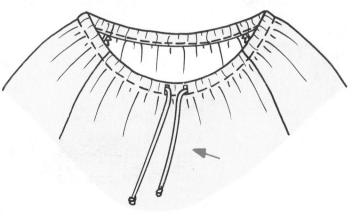

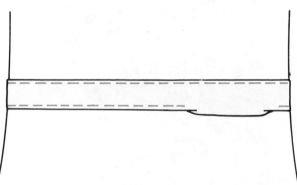

For an adjustable band under the bustline or around the waist, cut a strip of fabric for the casing 1″ (2 cm) wide and long enough to go around the gown where you are going to place the elastic. At the center front, make two vertical buttonholes 1/2″ (1.3 cm) apart so that you can adjust the tightness of the elastic with two ties.

Sew the ends of the band right sides together to form a circle. On the wrong side of the gown, pin the band where you want to place the elastic. Fold under the raw edges and sew a seam close to the edges all the way around the gown. Make two ties as described for the neck opening. Cut one length of elastic 10″ (26 cm) shorter than the measurement around your body. Refer to the neck opening for instructions on how to make the tie and how to insert it.

For a different look, you may want to have elastic around the elbow. Use the same method as described for the bust.

If you do not want to make spaghetti straps for the ties, you can use ready made bands. Also, around the bottom of the bustline, the waist, or the arm, you can use either bias tape or other types of banding rather than self-fabric.

Another variation for under the bustline or around the waist can be obtained by using stretch lace. Take a wide stretch lace, measure it around your waist so it feels comfortable. Put on the gown and mark your natural waistline. Sew the ends of the elastic lace together to form a circle. Divide the circle in fourths with pins. Sew two or three rows of gathering stitches under the position of the stretch lace. Divide the gown at the waistline in fourths with pins.

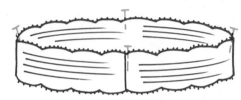

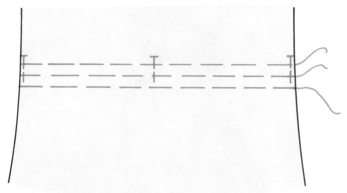

Place the wrong side of lace on the right side of the gown, the bottom edge of the lace should be on the bottom edge of the marked waistline. Pin the lace to the gown, matching the pins. Pull up gathering stitches to fit lace. Sew on the lace on both edges, using a zigzag stitch. Trim the fabric under the stretch lace.

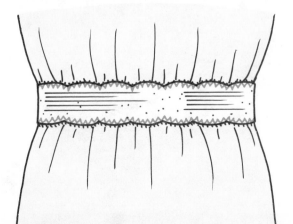

97

ELASTIC SHEERING:

Sheering is gathering with the use of elastic thread. When you use elastic thread, the elastic thread should be on the bobbin and regular thread on top. Use a stitch length slightly longer than medium.

If you would like to have the sheering at the waist, mark your natural waistline on the gown. Sew the first row following this marked line. Leave long enough ends at the side seam, so that the ends can be secured. Up from the waistline, sew as many lines as you desire. As you sew, you have to stretch the fabric to its original shape. Secure the threads at the side seams by making knots. This type of sheering is also very attractive under the bustline or at the ends of the sleeves.

APPLIQUES:

An easy method to personalize a gown is with the use of lace appliques. Cut out a design in a piece of lace. Tape the design to the skirt of the gown. Sew around the edge of the design with a close zigzag stitch.

Trim the tricot underneath the design. You can use more than one design, this depends upon the size of the design and your personal preference.

See the end of this section for various ways to hem a gown.

VIEW B

This gown can be made with or without elastic under the bustline. Trace off the pattern pieces No. 1 and No. 5. Tape the two pieces together as indicated on the pattern. The back and the front are identical. For the amount of fabric you need, see the following chart.

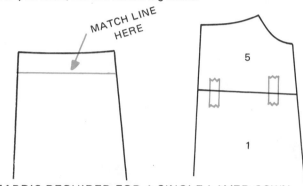

MATCH LINE HERE

FABRIC REQUIRED FOR A SINGLE LAYER GOWN FOR ALL SIZES

Fabric 96" (249 cm) to 108" (274 cm) Wide

long gown	1 1/2 yd (1.40 m)
Short gown	1 1/8 yd (1.05 m)

Fabric 45" (115 cm) Wide

long gown	3 yd (2.75 m)
short gown	2 1/4 yd (2.10 m)

Decide how the gown will be finished and purchase notions accordingly.

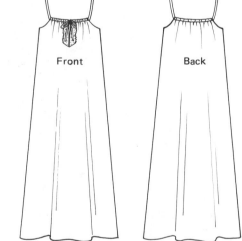

Front   Back

Place the fabric double, right side to right side. Cut out a back and a front. If you would like to have a lace decoration at the center front as illustrated, this should be done first. Cut a strip of lace 12" (31 cm) long. We recommend using a lace which is approximately 1½" to 2" (3.8 cm to 5 cm) wide with one of the sides straight. Mark the center front 6" (15 cm) down from the neckline. Place the lace at the center front with the straight edge at the center front. Be sure the lace matches on both sides.

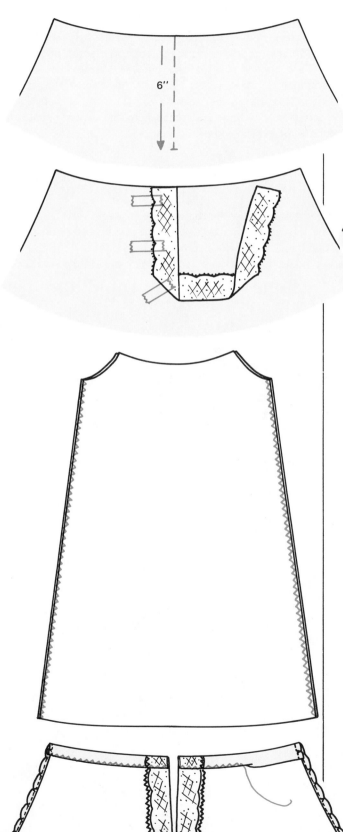

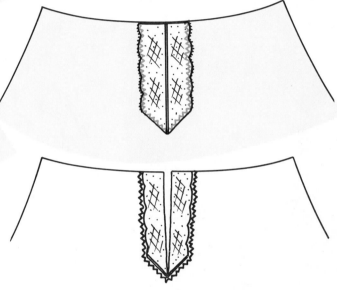

At the mark 6″ (15 cm) down, angle the corner by turning the lace under so that you have a right angle. Now turn up the remainder of the lace so that the straight edges meet at the center front. Using a small zigzag stitch, sew on the lace at the outer edge. Trim off the tricot on the wrong side close to the stitches. Trim off the under layer of lace at the point.

Place the back and the front, right side to right side, and sew the side seams. At the arm opening, turn a narrow hem to the wrong side and hem. If your machine has a blind hem stitch, use this for a very attractive hem.

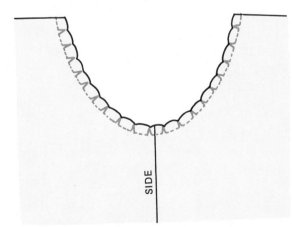

On the back and front at the neck opening, turn a hem to the wrong side ¾″ (2 cm). Turn under the raw edges and sew close to the edge. This will be the casing for the shoulder straps.

101

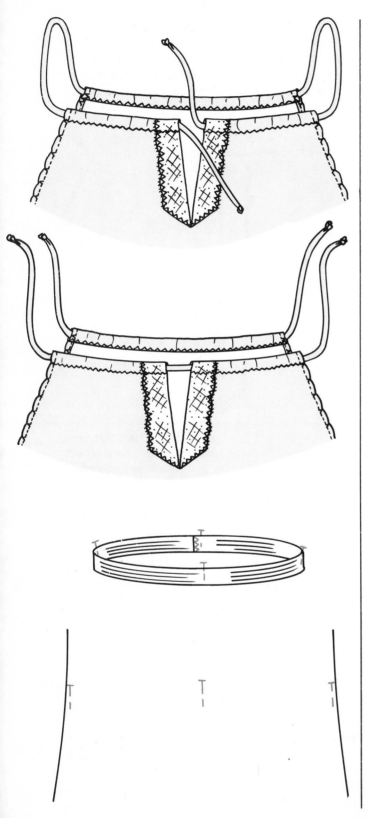

For the straps, cut a strip of fabric approximately 62" (157 cm) long and 1" (2.5 cm) wide. Fold the strip lengthwise, right side to right side. Sew a seam the length of the strip. Turn the band right side out (See Section II for Slips explaining an easy way to turn the bands). Insert the band starting at the center front. Continue through the casing at the back and through to the center front. Make a knot at each end of the band.

If you do not wish to tie the band at the center front, you can tie them on each shoulder. In this case instead of making one band, you make two bands. Insert one band in the casing in the back and one band in the casing in the front.

If you would like to have elastic underneath the bustline, put on the nightgown and mark the back and the front where you want to place the elastic. Stretch the elastic around your body so that it feels comfortable. Sew the ends of the elastic to form a circle. Divide the elastic in fourths with pins. Divide the gown in fourths with pins. Place the elastic on the wrong side of the gown matching the pins. Sew a seam on top of the elastic, stretching the elastic to fit the fabric.

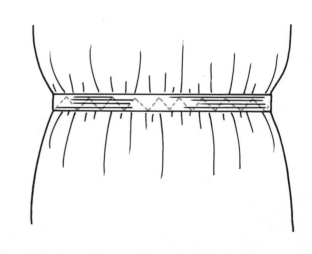

For hemming the gown, see the end of this section.

VIEW C

The top part of this nightgown can be made using either a single or double layer of fabric. You can use nylon tricot with a top layer of nylon sheer, nylon sheer as the bottom layer with the top layer of lace or just a single layer of nylon tricot.

The bottom part of the gown can be made using a single layer of tricot or tricot plus nylon sheer. If you are using nylon sheer for the overlayer, cut the front and back 4″ (10 cm) wider.

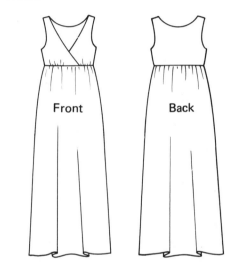

Front   Back

Trace off Pattern Pieces No. 1, 6 and 7. See the chart for the amount of fabric you need.

FABRIC REQUIRED FOR A SINGLE LAYER GOWN FOR ALL SIZES

Fabric 96″ (249 cm) to 108″ (274 cm) wide

Long Gown	1 3/4 yd (1.60m)
Short Gown	1 3/8 yd (1.30m)

Fabric 45″ (115cm) wide

Long Gown	3 1/8 yd (2.85m)
Short Gown	2 1/4 yd (2.10m)

Decide how the gown will be finished and purchase notions accordingly.

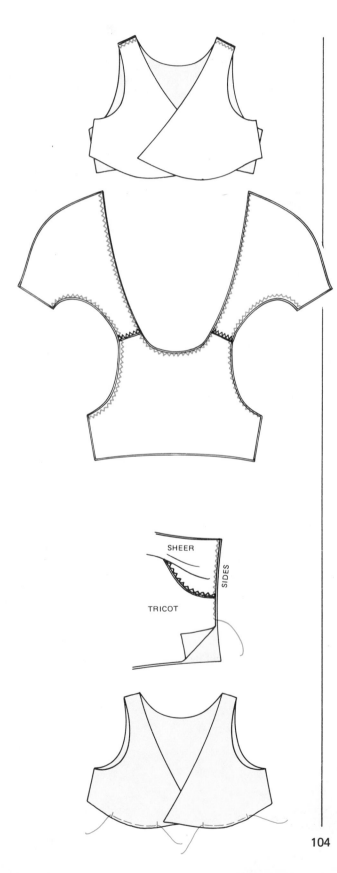

Place the fabric double, right side to right side, and cut out two of Pattern Piece No. 1, as the back and the front are identical. Cut out Pattern Pieces No. 6 and 7. If you are using a double layer for the bodice, cut these out at this time. Sew the shoulder seams by placing the back and the front, right side to right side. You sew the shoulder seam for each layer separately.

Place the nylon sheer bodice and nylon tricot bodice right side to right side. Sew the neck and the arm openings using a narrow seam allowance. Trim the seam allowance if you are using tricot and sheer. Turn right side out by pulling the front part through the shoulder.

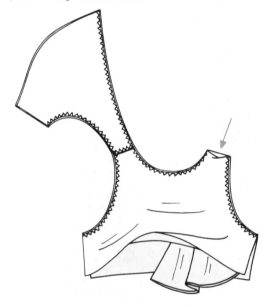

Sew the side seams, sewing each layer separately in one continuous operation.

At the bottom of the bodice of the gown between the two marks on the pattern piece, sew a gathering stitch; pull the bobbin thread and gather the fabric to a width of 3'' (7.5 cm). Tie the ends of the gathering thread securely. As nylon fabric is very slippery, it is important that the knot is tight. If you do not do this, there is a possibility that the gathering will fall apart.

Overlap the center front by overlapping the right side of the front over the left side so that the center front line meets. To keep the fabric in place, sew a seam as close as possible to the bottom edge. Sew the side seams for the skirt of the gown. If you are using double layers, sew the two skirts separately.

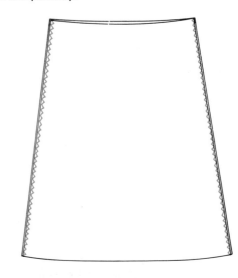

If you are using two layers, sew gathering stitches all the way around the top of the sheer skirt. Place the wrong side of the sheer skirt on the right side of the tricot skirt. Pull the gathering stitches to fit the tricot skirt; pin to hold in place. Sew gathering stitches all the way around the skirt through both layers of fabric, sew gathering stitches slightly below the gathering stitches on the sheer.

If you are using single layer for the skirt, sew gathering stitches all the way around the skirt. Place the top of the gown right side to right side with the skirt, matching the side seams, center front and center back. Gather the skirt to fit the bodice and sew the bodice to the skirt.

For a very pretty decoration on the bodice, sew a design using a very close zigzag stitch through both layers. On the inside, trim away the nylon tricot close to the stitches. Be careful so that you do not cut the nylon sheer.

106

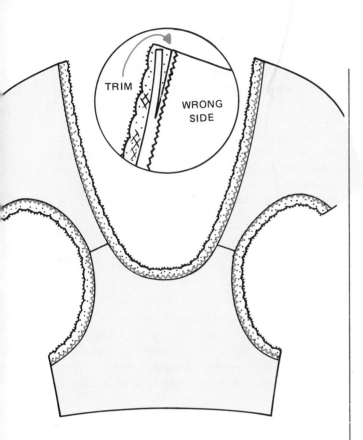

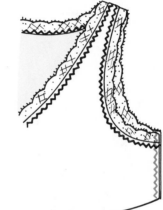

If you are using a single layer bodice, we suggest that you use a narrow lace to finish the neck and the arm openings. Start out by sewing the shoulder seams together. Overlap the lace on the right side ¼" (6 mm). Sew on the lace using a narrow zigzag stitch. Trim the fabric under the lace as close as possible to the stitches. After you have sewn the lace on the arm openings, sew the side seams. The rest of the construction for the gown is the same as previously described.

To finish around the neck and arm openings, here is another method which you may want to try. This method makes use of a band. When using a band, use the same fabric as you used for the nightgown. If you are using nylon tricot, you should make the band from nylon tricot. If you are using both nylon tricot and nylon sheer, the bands should be made from nylon sheer. Cut two bands for the arm opening and one band for the neck opening.

For the neck opening, cut one strip of fabric. For Size small, cut 38" (96 cm); Medium, cut 40"(101 cm); Large, cut 42 "(107cm); Extra Large, cut 44½" (113 cm) and 2" (5 cm) wide with the stretch going lengthwise. If you are using woven fabric, the strip should be cut on the bias. For the arm opening, cut two strips of fabric 17¾" (45 cm) for size Small; 18¾" (47.5 cm) for size Medium; 20" (51 cm) for size Large; and 21¾" (55 cm) for size Extra Large.

Sew the shoulder and side seams of the bodice.

Fold the armbands double, right sides together and sew a seam at the ends, making two circles.

Fold each circular band double lengthwise, wrong sides together. Divide each circle in fourths with pins; divide the arm openings in fourths with pins.

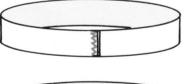

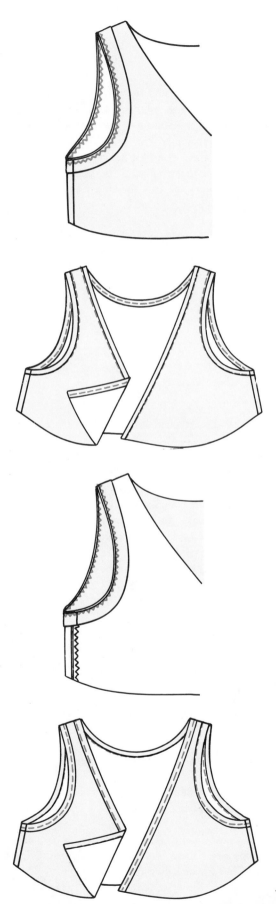

There are two different methods for sewing on the neckband and the armband. We will show you both of them.

Place armbands on right sides of arm openings, raw edges together, matching the pins. Line up seam in armband to side seam. Sew on band using ¼" (6 mm) seam allowance. Repeat above procedure for neck opening but do not sew the band into a circle. Start at the bottom of the center front and sew on the band all the way to the other side.

Finish the arm openings and the neck opening by folding the bands over the seam allowance to wrong side. Pin in place. Sew a straight stitch on the right side as close as possible to the band. (Stitch in the ditch.) Be sure to catch the band on the wrong side of the opening with your stitches.

The other method is to place the armband on the wrong side of the opening with the raw edges together and sew on the band using ¼" (6 mm) seam allowance.

Finish the arm and neck opening by folding the bands over the seam allowance to the right side. Topstitch from the right side close to the edge of the band.

See the end of this section for various ways to hem the gown.

VIEW D

Here is another simple nightgown you can construct using Pattern Pieces No. 1 and 8. Refer to the chart for the correct amount of fabric needed.

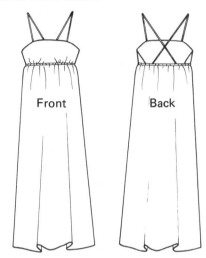

Front   Back

FABRIC REQUIRED FOR A SINGLE LAYER GOWN FOR ALL SIZES

Fabric 96″ (249 cm) to 108″ (274 cm) wide
long gown	1 1/2 yd (1.40m)
short gown	1 1/8 yd (1.05m)

Fabric 45″ (115 cm) wide
long gown	2 3/4 yd (2.55m)
short gown	2 yd (1.85m)

Decide how the gown will be finished and purchase notions accordingly.

Trace off Pattern Pieces 1 and 8. Fold the fabric right side to right side. Cut two pieces of No. 1 for the back and the front. On the bodice of the gown sew a gathering stitch between the marks on the pattern piece. Gather the fabric so that the width will be 3″ (7.5 cm) on each side between the marks.

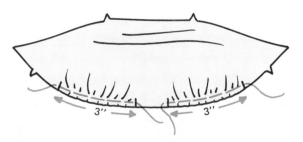

3″   3″

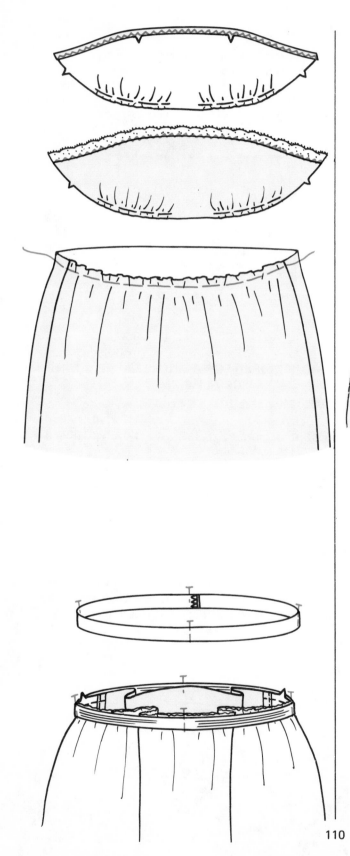

Turn a narrow hem to the wrong side and hem around the top edge. Or, you can use a narrow lace to finish the top edge.

Sew the side seams of the skirt. Sew a gathering stitch on the top of the front of the skirt. Pin the bodice to the skirt, matching the notches on the bodice with the side seam of the skirt. Gather the front skirt to fit the bodice.

Sew on the skirt to the bodice using a 3/8″ (1 cm) seam allowance. If you are using woven fabric, overcast the edges all the way around.

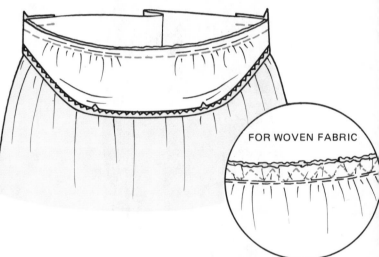

FOR WOVEN FABRIC

Stretch a piece of elastic under your bustline so that it feels comfortable. We recommend using 3/8″ (1 cm) elastic. Sew the ends of the elastic to form a circle. Divide the elastic in fourths with pins. Place the elastic on the wrong side of the fabric, edge to edge, with the top of the skirt. Match one pin in elastic to center front, second and third pin to side seams and fourth pin to center back. Sew a seam on top of the elastic, stretching the elastic between the pins to fit the fabric.

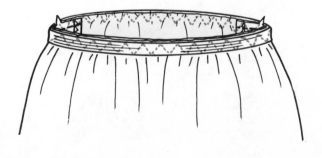

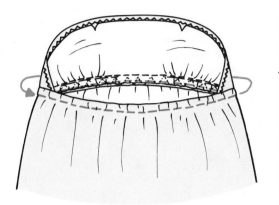

On the back, turn under the elastic and sew a seam on top of the elastic. Be sure to stretch the elastic when you are sewing the seam.

On the front, topstitch on the right side through the elastic with the seam allowance facing down. Be sure to stretch the elastic as you sew.

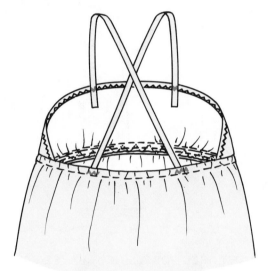

Make two spaghetti straps approximately 21'' (54 cm) long. To make spaghetti straps, see Section II for Slips. Sew on the end of each strap to the bodice at the mark indicated on the pattern. To obtain the correct length for the straps, put on the gown, cross the straps in the back and pick the length which is the most comfortable for you. Place the straps between the center back and the side seam. Sew on the strap to the back.

As a variation, you may want to decorate your gown with lace at the center front. You can use a wide lace or a number of strips of narrow lace. You can either leave the tricot underneath the lace or you can trim it. If you are using lace on the front, we suggest that you sew on the lace before you sew the side seams of the skirt.

See the end of this section on how to finish the bottom hem.

VIEW E

View E is a slight variation of View D. The difference is in the bodice. Trace off Pattern Pieces No. 1 and 9. Refer to the chart for the correct amount of fabric needed.

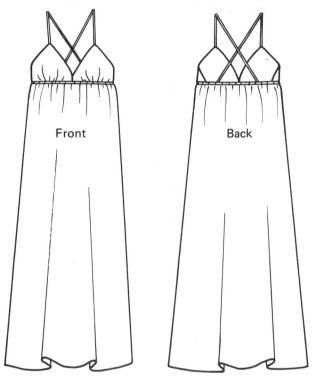

Front   Back

FABRIC REQUIRED FOR A SINGLE LAYER GOWN FOR ALL SIZES

Fabric 96" (249 cm) to 108" (274 cm) wide

long gown	1 3/8 yd (1.30 m)
short gown	1 yd (0.95 m)

Fabric 45" (115 cm) wide

long gown	2 3/4 yd (2.55 m)
short gown	2 yd (1.85 m)

Decide how the gown will be finished and purchase notions accordingly.

Fold the fabric double and cut out two of Pattern Piece No. 1 for the front and the back. Cut out Pattern Piece No. 9. The top can be made using either one or two layers of fabric. The edges around the bra can be finished in various ways. You can use a narrow lace, overlap the lace ¼" (6 mm) on the right side of the bra. Miter the lace at the shoulder strap placement. Sew on the lace using a close zigzag stitch. Trim the tricot under the lace close to the stitches.

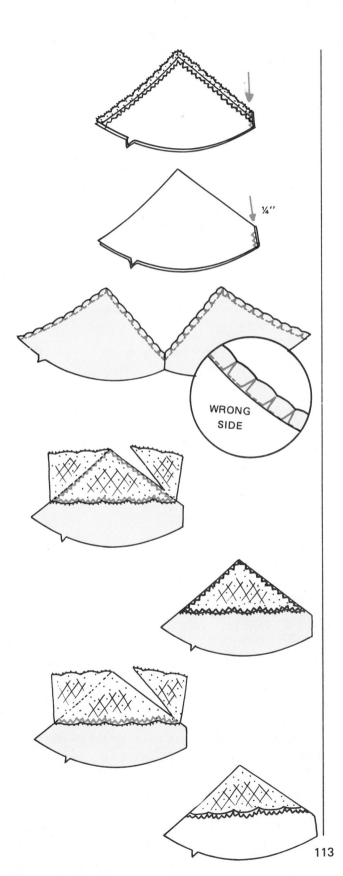

Now, sew the two cups together at the center front.

Or, you may prefer to finish the edges using a blind hem. This gives a scalloped effect. Start by sewing the center front seam of the cups, sew from bottom edge to within ¼″ (6 mm) from top edge. Fold the hem to the wrong side ¼″ (6 mm) and sew the edge. Or, you can turn the hem to the wrong side and finish the edges with a straight stitch.

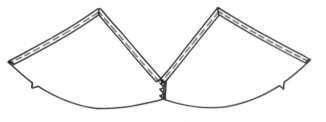

Another variation is to have half the bra made of lace. Place a wide piece of lace over the top part of the bra. Sew on the lace on the outside edges of the tricot. Sew the bottom of the lace through the tricot. Trim off the lace at the edges.

If you wish to trim off the tricot under the lace only, sew the lace at the bottom. Trim off the lace even with the outside edge of the tricot. Trim the tricot from under the lace.

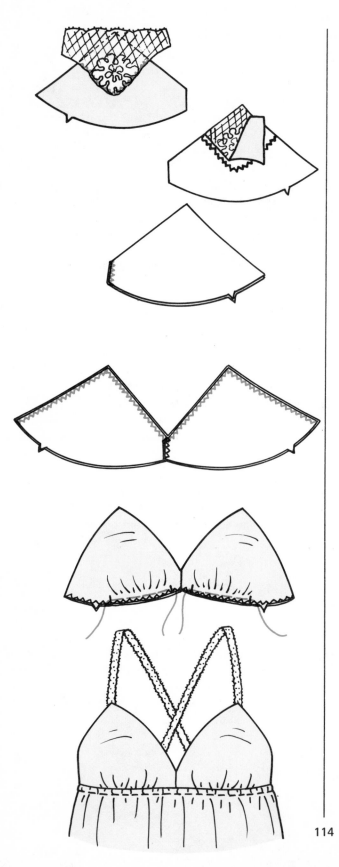

Or you can use a lace motif from wide lace to decorate the cups. Tape or pin lace to cup with right sides up. Stitch lace to cup along the outline of the motif at the bottom edge. Trim the lace even with the edges of the cup. Trim the tricot from under the cups.

If you plan to use two layers of fabric for the bra, sew the center front on both layers. Place the two layers, right side to right side, sew around the bra, leaving the bottom edge open. Turn right side out. To facilitate handling, sew the bottom edges together.

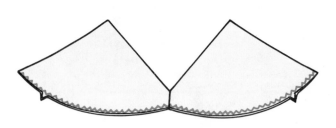

Sew a gathering stitch on the bottom of the bra between the marks shown on the pattern piece. Gather the fabric so that it is 3" (7.5 cm) wide.

The rest of the construction is the same as described for View D. Instead of using spaghetti straps for the shoulder bands, you may use a narrow lace.

114

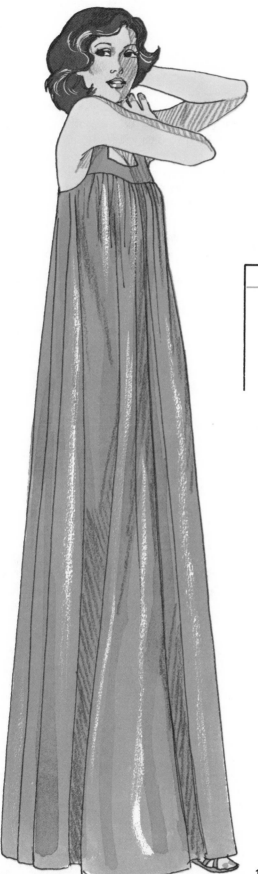

VIEW F

View F is a nightgown with a front and back yoke. Trace off two patterns of No. 1 and one Pattern No. 10 and 11. Trace off Pattern Pieces No. 12 and 13. Cut out the pattern pieces. Tape Pattern Piece No. 10 to No. 1 on the line indicated on the pattern. This is for the front of the gown. For the back of the gown, tape Pattern Piece No. 11 to the other No. 1 pattern piece. Refer to the chart for the correct amount of fabric needed.

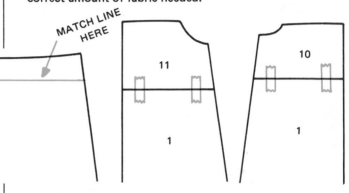

MATCH LINE HERE

FABRIC REQUIRED FOR A SINGLE LAYER GOWN FOR ALL SIZES

Fabric 96'' (249 cm) to 108'' (274 cm) wide

long gown	1 1/2 yd (1.40 m)
short gown	1 1/8 yd (1.05 m)

Fabric 45'' (115 cm) wide

long gown	3 1/8 yd (2.85 m)
short gown	2 3/8 yd (2.20 m)

Decide how the gown will be finished and purchase notions accordingly.

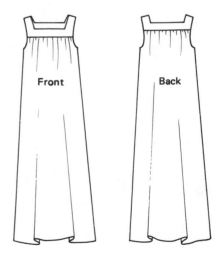

Front   Back

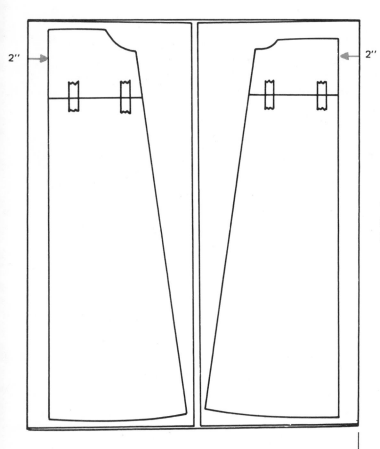

2"

2"

Yokes can be made using a single layer of fabric or a double layer. For example, the inside yoke can be made with tricot and the outside with sheer. You can use two layers of sheer with lace in between, or the outside yoke can be made with lace and the inside yoke with sheer.

The skirt part can be constructed using a single layer of fabric or, if using tricot, you can have an overlay of sheer. You can also use non-stretch fabric to construct this gown.

If you are using an overlayer of sheer, we suggest that you cut the sheer wider than the underlayer. This gives the gown a fuller appearance. When cutting out the fabric, place the front edge 2" (5 cm) from the fold of the fabric.

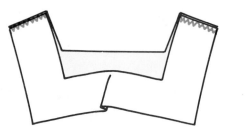

DOUBLE YOKE:

Sew the shoulder seams of the two layers of fabric separately.

Place the right sides together at the neckline. Sew around the neckline. Clip to each corner. If desired understitch the seam allowance to the inside yoke. Turn the yoke right side out.

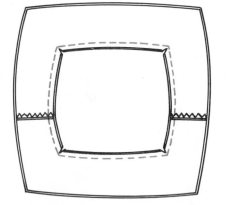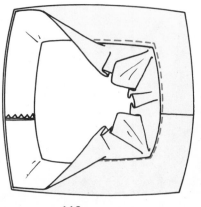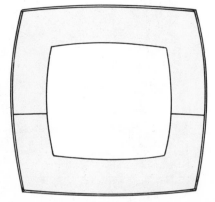

A

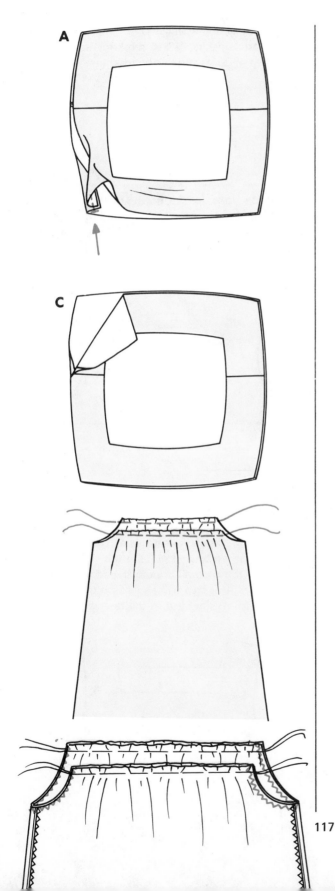

Finish the arm openings of the yoke. Place the inside and outside yokes, right sides together, at the front arm opening. Stitch from the yoke seam to the shoulder seam, turning the yoke wrong side out as you sew. Clip the seam allowance and turn the front arm opening right side out.

B

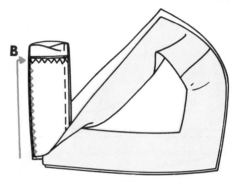

Place the inside and outside yokes, right sides together, at the back arm opening. Stitch from the yoke seam to the shoulder, turning the yoke wrong side out as you sew. Clip the seam allowance. Repeat for the other arm opening.

D

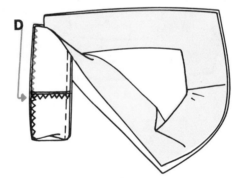

Sew the side seams of the gown together. Sew a gathering seam around the top edge of the gown using long stitches.

If you are using two layers of fabric, sew the side seams of the sheer and the tricot separately. Sew the gathering seams on the top of the gowns separately.

Finish the arm opening by placing the two layers, right side to right side, and sew around the arm openings. Turn right side out. If you wish, you can topstitch around the arm opening close to the edges.

C

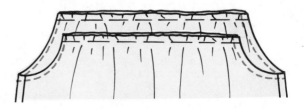

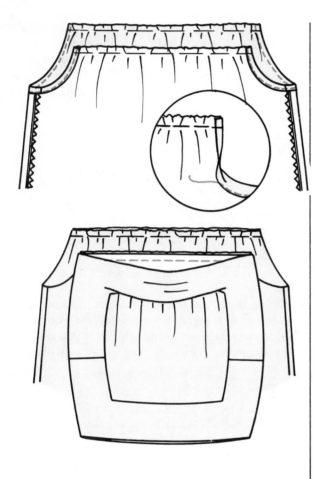

If you are constructing a single layer gown, fold the raw edges of the arm opening ¼" (6 mm) to the wrong side, fold under the raw edges and sew by machine.

Pin the outside yoke to the gown, right sides together, matching the center front, center back and the edges of the arm opening. Gather the gown to fit the yoke. Adjust the gathers evenly. Sew the front and the back yoke seams. Press the seam allowance towards the yoke.

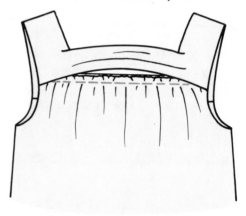

Pin the inside yoke over the seam allowance. On the right side, stitch in the ditch, being sure to catch the inside yoke with your stitches. Or if you are using fabric that ravels, fold the raw edges under and pin. On the right side, stitch in the ditch or topstitch all around the edges of the yoke close to the edges. This step will also attach the inside yoke. Or, you may wish to simply turn the raw edges under and stitch by hand.

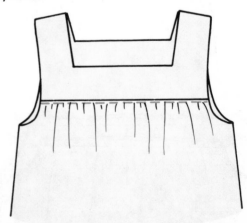

SINGLE LAYER YOKE:

A yoke can be cut from a single layer of fabric or a double layer of fabric treated as a single layer yoke. For example: If the outside yoke is cut from lace and the inside yoke is cut from sheer, place pieces together and stitch around all the raw edges and treat as one piece of fabric. Sew the shoulder seams of the yoke.

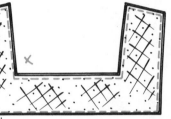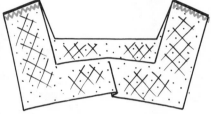

Use narrow lace to finish around the neck and the arm openings. Place the lace on the right side of the openings. Line up the edge of the lace with the raw edges of the fabric. Miter the lace at the corners. Sew the lace on the inside edge of the lace using a zigzag stitch. Trim the excess nylon from the wrong side close to the stitches. Stitch across the mitered corners. Trim excess lace from the wrong side close to the stitches.

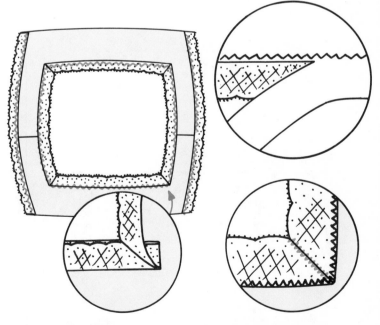

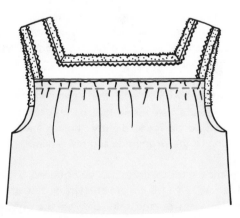

Sew the side seams and finish the arm openings and gather the top edge of the gown as previously described. Pin to the yoke, right side to right side, matching the center front, the center back, and the edges of the arm opening. Adjust the gathers evenly to fit the yoke. Sew the yoke seams.

119

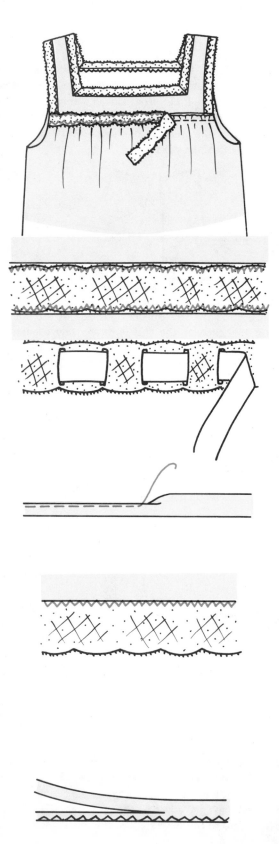

Another way of sewing the gown to the yoke is to place the yoke and the gown, wrong sides together. Now the seam shows on the right side. To hide the seam and at the same time to add an extra touch to the nightgown, place a narrow lace on top of the yoke seam and sew both edges of the lace.

If you would like to obtain a more colorful effect, you can use a piece of colored ribbon the same width as the lace. Place the ribbon under the lace and sew them on close to the edge.

Or, you can use insertion lace. Take a narrow piece of colored ribbon the same width as the holes in the lace and thread the holes with the ribbon. You can either gather the lace or it can lie flat.

HEMMING:

The bottom of a nightgown can be finished in a great variety of ways. You can simply fold the hem to the wrong side, fold under the raw edges and stitch by machine. Or, you can finish the bottom edge with lace if you are using nylon tricot or nylon sheer. You can use whichever width of lace you desire. It is not necessary to use the same color lace as the color of the garment. You may wish to use a lace of a contrasting color. See Section I for instructions on how to apply lace.

If you are using two layers for the nightgown, we suggest that you finish the hem using lace on the top layer. The underlayer should be made slightly shorter and finish the hem by rolling to the wrong side and sew a hem.

Or, a very nice smooth finish can be obtained if you fold the nylon tricot ½″ (1.3 cm) to the wrong side and sew a narrow zigzag seam on the fold. Sew on the right side of the fabric with the right hand swing of the needle barely missing the fabric. Trim off the excess fabric very close to the stitches.

If your sewing machine can sew a blind stitch, use this stitch instead of the zigzag stitch and you will get a scalloped edge. You obtain the nicest scalloped effect if you set your machine for a wide zigzag, and slightly tighten the top tension. Before you use this method, try it on a piece of scrap fabric so that you get the effect most pleasing to you. This is one time when you have the garment to the right of the needle, as this seam was designed for blind hemming and the swing to make the blind hem is from the right to the left.

STRETCH

An easy way to finish the bottom edge of a gown is to use lettuce edging. Set the sewing machine for a very close stitch length. Set the zigzag control for a width slightly wider than medium. Stretch the edge of the fabric as tightly as you can and sew over the edges.

Lace can be used in a variety of ways at the bottom of a gown. You can have a wide lace at the bottom and two or three strips of lace above the bottom layer. It looks very attractive if each strip is narrower than the one beneath it. Use a small zigzag stitch to sew on the lace and cut away the fabric underneath the lace.

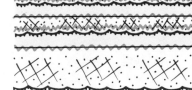

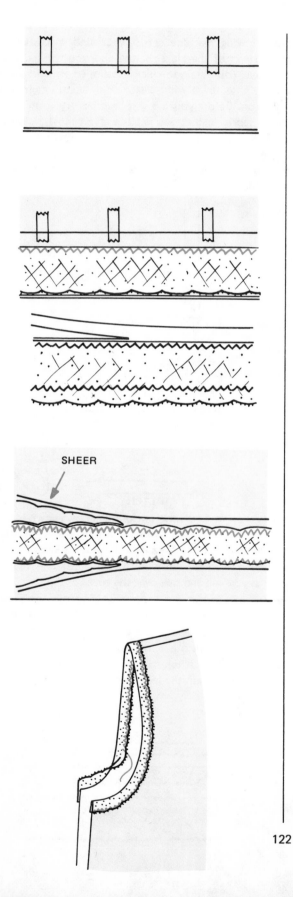

A very attractive way to use lace above the hemline or at the hemline is to use sheer under the lace. Cut the sheer the same length and a little wider than the lace. First tape the sheer to the garment, place the lace on top of the sheer, right side up and sew the top edge of the lace through all three layers. Cut away the tricot from under the sheer.

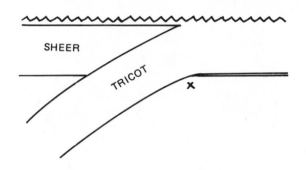

Sew another seam ¼" (6 mm) up from the bottom edge of the lace through the lace and the sheer. Trim the sheer close to the stitches on both the upper and lower edges of the lace.

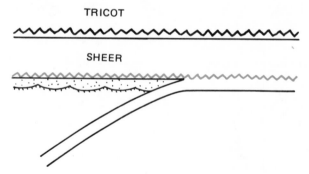

If you are placing the lace above the hemline and you wish to line the lace with sheer, place the sheer on the garment and place the lace on top of the sheer. Sew the lace and the sheer on the garment at both the bottom and the top of the lace. Cut the tricot from under the lace. Trim the sheer close to the stitches on the right side.

Another method for finishing both the hem and the arm openings is to select a piece of lace with the same design on both sides. Fold the lace double lengthwise and insert the raw edges of the hem and the arm openings into the lace. Sew on the lace. Be sure to catch the lace on both sides.

SHADOW LACE:

Cut a strip of sheer twice the width of the lace plus the seam allowance. Fold the sheer double lengthwise, wrong sides together. Enclose the lace in the folded sheer band. Pin the right side of the lace on the right side of the garment and sew along the top edge of the lace. Trim the sheer close to the stitches.

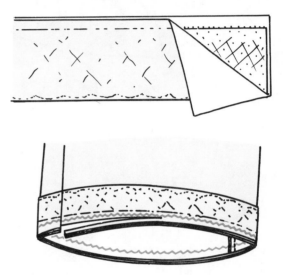

RUFFLE HEM:

When you are making a double ruffled hem, you have to be sure to deduct one-half the width of the ruffle strip from the length of the gown. Cut a strip of fabric approximately 13'' (33 cm) wide or as wide as desired and 1½ times the width of the bottom of the gown. Sew the ends together, right side to right side, to form a circle. Fold the circle double lengthwise, wrong sides together. At ¼'' (6 mm) from the raw edges, sew a gathering seam. Divide the ruffle and the bottom of the gown into fourths with pins. Pin the ruffle to the wrong side of the gown, matching pins. Adjust the gathers evenly between the pins. Sew on the ruffle.

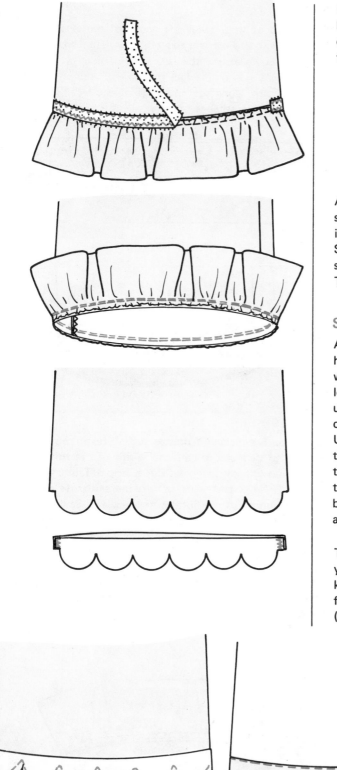

On the right side, use a piece of lace or a finished decorative band and sew this over the seam on both edges of the lace or band. If you are using lace, we suggest that you cut away the fabric under the lace.

Another way to apply the ruffle is to place the ruffle, right side to right side, with the bottom edge of the gown, matching the pins. Adjust the gathers evenly between the pins. Sew on the ruffle using ¼" (6 mm) seam allowance. Sew a second seam close to the first seam on the seam allowance. Trim the seam allowance close to the stitches.

SCALLOPED EDGE:

A scalloped edge is very attractive at the bottom of the hemline. Excluding the seam allowances, measure the width of the hemline. Divide the length into as many scallops as you wish to have. The size of the scallops depends upon your personal taste. Mark a few scallops on a piece of paper. Cut out the scallops and use these as a pattern. Using this pattern, cut out the scallops on the bottom of the gown. Cut a facing for the scallops 1" (2.5 cm) deeper than the depth of the scallop. Sew the ends of the facing together and sew the side seams. Pin the facing to the bottom edge, right side to right side. Sew around the edges and clip the seam allowance.

Turn the facing to the wrong side and lightly press. Now you can either topstitch the straight edge of the facing to keep it in place or you can sew a nice decorative stitch, following the outline of the scallops approximately ½" (1.3 cm) from the edge. Trim away the excess fabric.

124

robes

You can use a great variety of fabrics for robes, from very sheer to quilted fabric. The weight of the robe will depend upon the season and the climate. You may wish to have a robe of nylon tricot for the summer, brushed nylon for the spring and fall and stretch terrycloth for the winter months. You can vary the length of the sleeves and the length of the gown according to your personal preference.

We will start out with a basic robe pattern with set-in sleeves, buttons at the front and a regular collar. Later on in this section, we will explain how you can easily make variations for a new look.

Fold the fabric double, right side to right side. If you are using stretch fabric, make sure the greatest degree of stretch goes around the body. Cut out the fabric. Mark the front folding line. Place the front and the back, right side to right side, and sew the shoulder seams.

Sew the sleeves in place before you sew the side seams and the sleeve seams. Match the notch on the cap of the sleeve with the shoulder seam. Match the edges of the sleeve with the underarm edges.

125

Sew sleeves and side seams in one operation starting at the bottom of the robe then down the sleeve seam.

Place collar pieces right sides together and sew seams on three sides, leaving neckline edge open. Turn right side out.

In order to keep the undercollar from showing, open up the collar, place the seam allowance towards the under-collar and topstitch close to the seam through the seam allowance. (You end up sewing through three layers.) This is called understitching. The understitched side of the collar will be the undercollar.

Pin the undercollar to the right side of the neck opening, matching the center of the collar to the center back. Match the notches on the collar to the shoulder seams. The ends of the collar should meet at the center front.

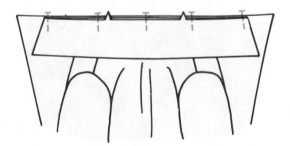

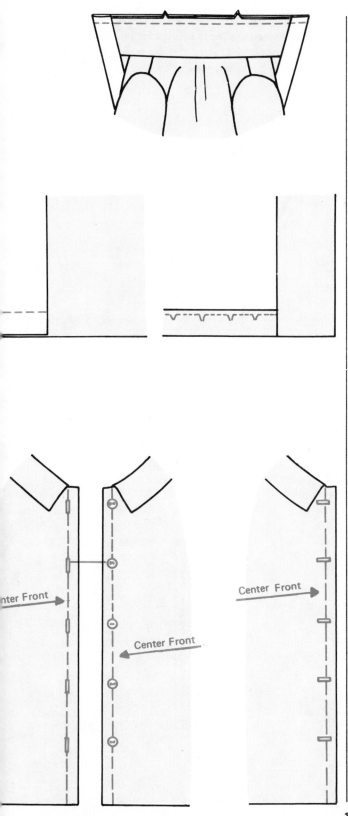

Fold the center front facing on the folding line to the right side, over collar. Sew the collar and the facing to the robe in one operation. Turn the facing to the wrong side.

After determining the desired hemline, attach the bottom edge of the facing by turning the right side of the facing to the right side of the robe. Sew a straight seam across the facing at the desired hemline. Turn the facing to the wrong side.

Hem the robe either by machine or by hand. If your sewing machine has a blind hem stitch, use it as the stitches will not show on the right side and it is faster than sewing the hem by hand.

Make as many buttonholes on the right side as you desire. If you are using non-stretch fabric, make horizontal buttonholes. If you are making the robe in stretch fabric, we recommend making vertical buttonholes. As there is less stretch going up and down, the buttonholes will be less likely to stretch out of shape. The buttonholes should always be approximately 1/8" (3 mm) larger than the button.

If you have made vertical buttonholes, remember to place the button 1/8" (3 mm) from the top of the buttonhole. This will assure you of an even line on the bottom of the garment.

127

If you are using a lightweight fabric for the robe, reinforce the buttonhole by placing a piece of interfacing or a piece of woven fabric between the facing and the front under the buttonholes. Sew the buttons on the left front.

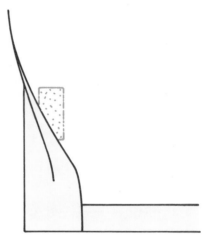

FRONT VARIATIONS:

If you would like to have a zipper at the center front, cut away the facing at the folding line. Use at least a 22'' (56 cm) long zipper. If you can purchase a longer zipper, it is better because then you can easily step into the robe instead of having to pull it on over your head. Place the zipper at the center front with the top of the zipper pull ½'' (1.3 cm) down from the neckline. Mark with a pin the end of the zipper.

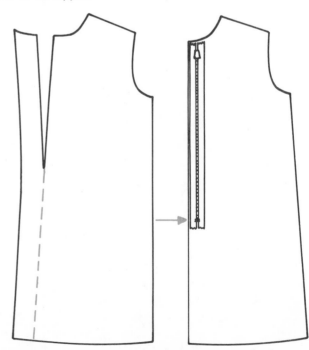

128

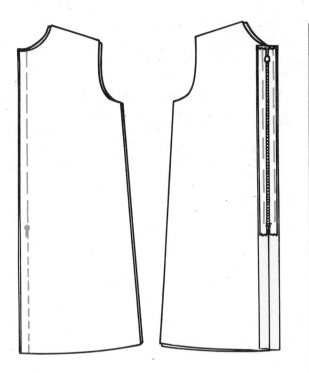

Pin the center front seam, right sides together. Sew, using a 5/8″ (1.5 cm) seam allowance. Sew from the bottom edge of the robe to the mark for end of the zipper; lock stitches; baste from the mark to the neckline. Press the seam allowance open.

Place the closed zipper, face down, on the wrong side, on the opened seam allowance. Place the middle of the zipper teeth along the basted seam. The top of the zipper pull should be ½″ (1.3 cm) down from the neckline. Baste the zipper in place, be sure that you baste the zipper only to the seam allowance. This will keep the zipper in place for sewing.

It is easier and faster to tape the zipper in position on the seam allowance. Place the tape across the zipper at about 3″ (7.5 cm) intervals.

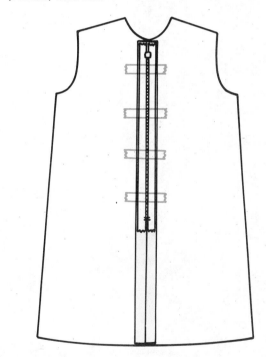

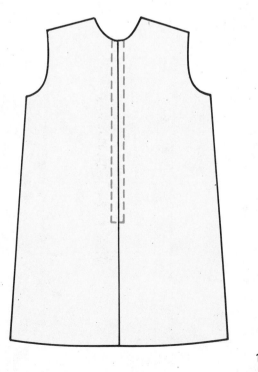

On the right side, using a zipper foot, sew ¼″ (6 mm) from the seam. Sew from the neckline to the end of the zipper and across the bottom of the zipper to the seam. Repeat for the other side. Remove the tape and the center front basting.

FRONT TRIMMING:

When you are using a zipper at the center front, you can use vertical strips of other colors to give a very attractive look. For example: If you would like to have two strips on each side of the zipper and you would like to have the strips 1¼'' (3.2 cm) wide, cut away from the center front of the pattern 2¼'' (5.7 cm) from the neckline to the bottom of the robe. Now cut two strips of fabric in the same color, the length of the robe and 1¾'' (4.5 cm) wide, this allows for a ¼'' (6 mm) seam allowance.

Cut two strips of fabric in another color 3'' (7.5 cm) wide. Place the wide strips, right side to right side. Leave an opening for the length of the zipper and from this point down, sew a seam in the middle of the strips. Fold each strip wrong side to wrong side. Now place one narrow strip on each side, right side to right side, and sew them to the wide strips.

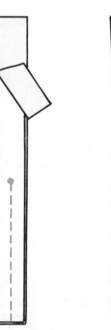

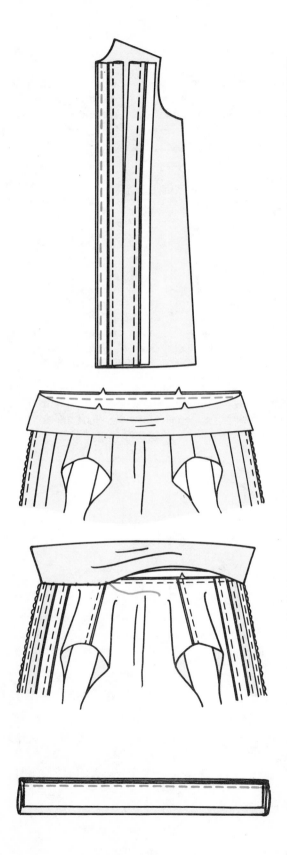

Sew the front of the robe to the strips, right side to right side. Insert a zipper at the center front.

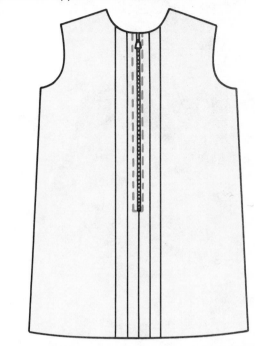

Construct the collar as previously described. Pin the under-collar to the right side of the neckline with the ends of the collar at the edges of front. Sew on the under collar to the neckline.

Press seam allowance toward the collar. Fold under the seam allowance of the upper collar and pin covering neckline seam. Stitch in place by hand.

When using strips at the front, it is very attractive to use the same color strips at the bottom of the sleeves. We suggest that you sew on the strips before you sew the sleeve seams. The widest strip should be at the bottom of the sleeve as this strip will be on the bottom edge of the sleeve. Fold the widest strip double, wrong sides together. Pin the other strip, right side and raw edges together and sew them together. Now sew the strip to the sleeves.

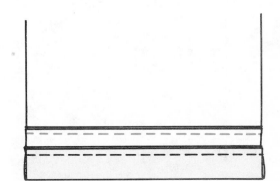

NECKLINES:

If you wish to have a simple round neck, you have to make a special facing. On the back and front of the pattern pieces, measure in 2" (5 cm) and draw a line, following the neck-line, from the shoulder to the center front and the center back. These pieces are the facings.

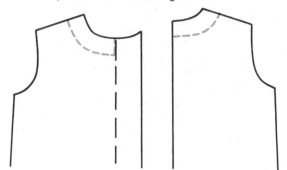

For the back facing, place the center back of the facing on a fold. Cut two front facings. Sew the back facing to the front facing at the shoulder seam, right side to right side. Sew the shoulder seam on the robe.

Fold the front facing on the folding line, right side to right side. Pin the facing for the neck opening, right side to right side. Sew on the facing.

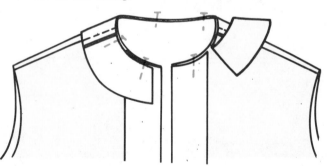

Fold the facing to the wrong side. Secure the ends of the front facing with a few hand stitches. You can topstitch around the neck opening or you can use decorative stitches.

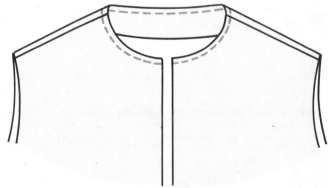

NECKLINE WITH LACE:

A round neckline looks very attractive when you use lace. We suggest that you make this type of robe from tricot and the front of the robe be left open just meeting at the center front with ties at the neckline.

The front part of the robe can be cut double or you can use a facing. If you plan to make the front double, cut each front by placing the center front line on the fold.

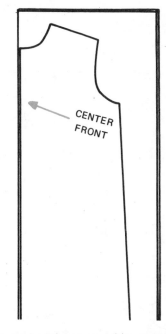

Fold each front double, wrong sides together and sew a seam at the neckline to facilitate handling. Sew the shoulders through the three layers of fabric.

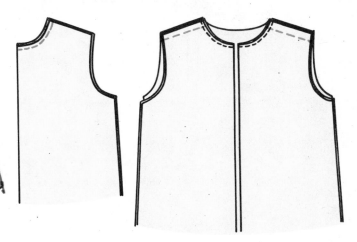

133

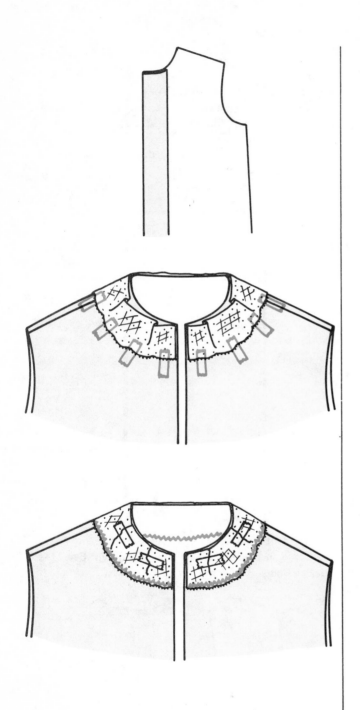

If you are using a single layer for the front, fold the front facing on the folding line on the wrong side. Sew across the facing at the neckline to keep it in place.

Pin or tape a strip of wide lace on the neckline, the straight edge of the lace should be placed edge to edge with the raw edges. The ends of the lace should be at the center front. So that the lace will lie smoothly around the neck, cut slits in the lace. If the lace has a flower design, try to cut the slits so that they follow the outline of one of the flowers.

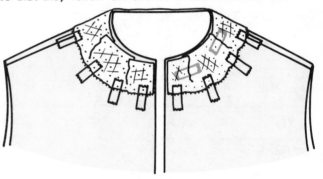

Overlap the slits in the lace so the lace is laying flat on the neckline. Pin or tape in place. Sew the lace to the robe along the inner edge of the lace. Trim the tricot under the lace close to the stitches. Sew the slits in place, following the outline of the design where you cut. Cut away the excess lace on the wrong side.

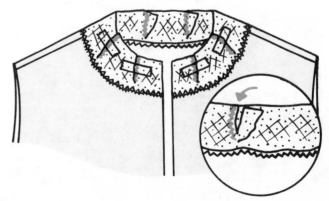

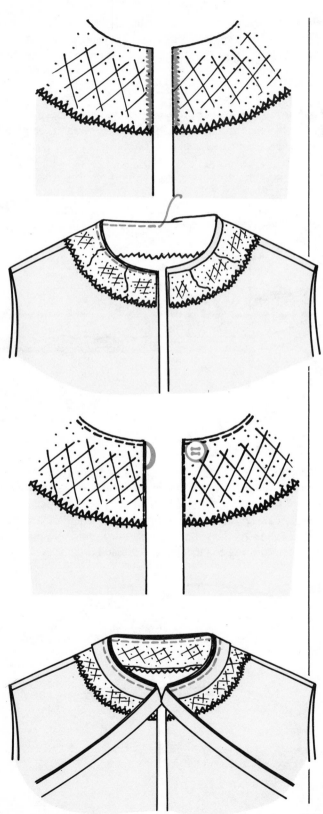

Stitch over the raw edges of the front edge of lace, using a medium zigzag stitch and a very short stitch length.

If you do not plan to cut away the tricot under the lace, then you have to place the edge of the lace ¼'' (6 mm) away from the edge. Fold this ¼'' (6 mm) under the lace and sew the edge close to the fold. This gives you a nice professional looking finish.

You can add a thread loop and a button at the neckline.

If you have cut away the tricot under the lace, we suggest that you finish the neckline with self-fabric binding. It looks very attractive if you use ties at the center front. For the binding, cut a piece of tricot 2'' (5 cm) wide the length of the neckline plus 40'' (102 cm) for the ties.

Fold the binding double lengthwise, wrong sides together. Make a mark 20'' (51 cm) from one end. Place this mark at the center front on one side. Pin the binding to the right side of the neckline, edge to edge, with the lace. Sew on the binding using a ¼'' (6 mm) seam allowance.

135

Finish the neckline by folding the binding over the seam allowance to the wrong side, and pin in place. Sew a straight stitch from the right side as close as possible to the seam, making sure your stitches catch the binding on the wrong side.

Fold in the raw edges of the neckband ties and topstitch to finish. If your machine has a blind stitch, sew this seam on both edges to obtain a scalloped finish.

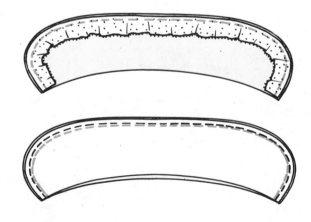

COLLAR WITH LACE EDGE:

Place the lace on the right side of one collar, place the straight edge of the lace along the outer rounded edges of the collar. Sew on the lace using a narrow seam allowance. Pin the collars, right sides and raw edges together. Sew the collars following the same stitching line as used for applying the lace. Turn the collar right side out and press.

NECKLINE WITH RUFFLE:

You may wish to finish the neck opening with a ruffle. Cut the fabric for the ruffle twice as long as the neck opening. The ruffle can be any width. It can be made from a single piece of fabric or from a double piece. For a double ruffle 1½ (3.8 cm) wide, cut a strip of fabric 3½" (9 cm) wide. For a single ruffle, cut a strip of fabric 2" (5 cm) wide.

If you are making a double ruffle, fold the fabric double lengthwise, right sides together. Sew across the ends, turn the fabric right side out and press. If you are making a single ruffle, make a narrow hem on one edge and the ends. For the hem, you can use either a close zigzag stitch, a blind hem stitch or lettuce edging when using stretch fabric.

If you are using non-stretch fabric, fold a very narrow double hem to the wrong side and sew.

On the raw edge of the fabric strip, sew a row of gathering stitches ¼" (6 mm) in from the edge. Divide the ruffle and the neck opening into fourths with pins. Pin the ruffle to the neckline with the right sides together, matching the pins; the ends of the ruffle band should be at the folding line. Gather the ruffle by pulling the bobbin thread. Adjust the gathers evenly to fit the neckline. Sew on the ruffle on top of the gathering stitches.

Finish the neckline with facing as previously described.

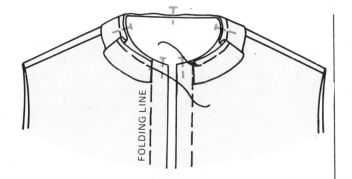

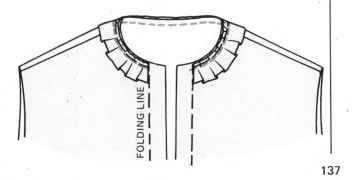

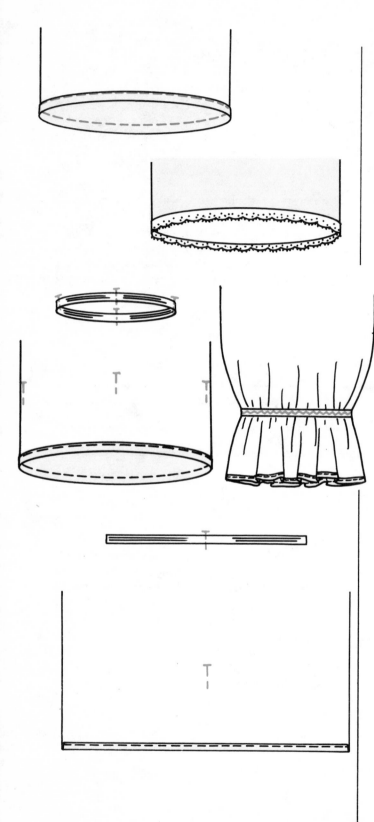

SLEEVES:

Regardless of the length of the sleeve, they can all be finished in the same way. You can use any of the methods described for finishing the hem of the gown such as scallops, lace, etc. Or, you can use elastic to obtain a ruffled edge. First, finish the bottom edge either by rolling a narrow hem to the wrong side or finish the edge with a narrow lace.

Measure a piece of narrow elastic around your arm where the sleeve will end. Be sure not to have too loose a fit as the elastic will stretch a little when you sew it to the sleeve. Cut two lengths of elastic and sew them together to form two circles. Divide the elastic circles in fourths with pins. Decide how wide you want the ruffled edge. At this point, divide the sleeve opening into fourths using pins. Pin the elastic to the wrong side of the sleeve, matching the pins. Stretch the elastic between the pins and using a zigzag stitch, sew on top of the elastic.

Another way to sew on the elastic which is easier, especially if you have a narrow sleeve, is to sew on the elastic before you sew the sleeve seam. Divide the elastic in half with a pin. Divide the sleeve in half. Pin the elastic to the wrong side of the sleeve, matching the pins. Sew on the elastic, stretching the elastic to fit the fabric. Now sew the sleeve seam.

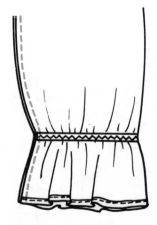

138

TRUMPET SLEEVE:

You can easily change a pattern to give you a trumpet sleeve. Cut out the sleeve pattern. Draw a line across the sleeve at the underarm. Draw a line in the middle of the sleeve from this line to the bottom of the sleeve. Draw a line halfway between the center line and the sleeve seam on each side. Cut the line open at the underarm. Cut the other lines open from the bottom of the sleeve to within 1/8" (3 mm) from the first line.

Place a piece of paper under the pattern. Tape the bottom of the sleeve to the top of the sleeve at the underarm. Spread the pattern apart the amount of flare desired.

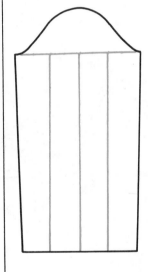

SLEEVE WITH CUFF:

This type of cuff looks best on a three quarters length sleeve. You may wish to widen the bottom of the sleeve to give it more fullness. Draw a straight line from the top of the underarm to a point 1" (2.5 cm) out from the bottom edge of the sleeve.

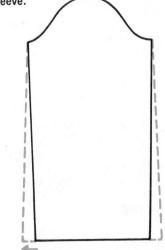

Sew the sleeve seams. Sew a gathering stitch on the bottom edge of the sleeve. Measure around the widest part of your forearm and add ½'' (1.3 cm) for seam allowance. The width of the cuff depends upon personal preference. For a finished cuff of 2'' (5 cm) wide, cut two pieces of fabric 5'' (13 cm). Sew the ends together, right side to right side, to form a circle. Fold the cuff double, lengthwise, wrong sides together. Divide the cuff in fourths with pins. Divide the bottom edge of the sleeve in fourths with pins. Pin the cuff to the sleeve, right side to right side, matching the pins. Gather the sleeve to fit the cuff and sew on the cuff.

PATCH POCKETS:

Pockets are always handy and add a finished look to your robe. They are very easy to construct. Just remember to take into consideration the weight of the fabric with which you are working. When you use a fine fabric, you can double the fabric in order to get sufficient strength.

The size of the pocket is a matter of personal preference. The average size of a finished pocket is approximately 6½'' (16.5 cm) long by 6¼'' (16 cm) wide.

For the pocket in lightweight fabric, cut the fabric twice the height of the pocket size. In this case, cut the pocket 14'' (35.5 cm) long and 7¼'' (18.5 cm) wide allowing a ½'' (1.3 cm) seam allowance.

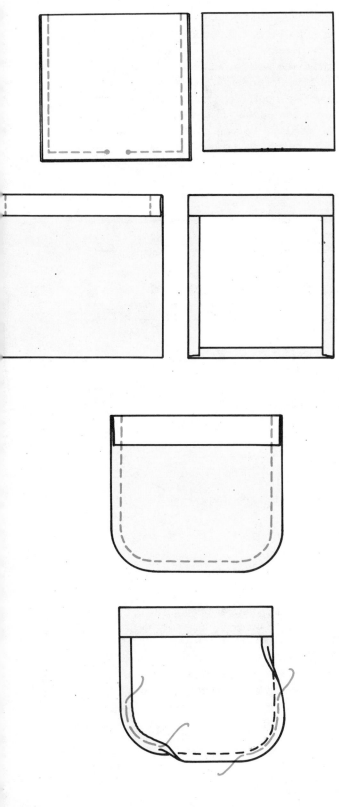

Double the fabric lengthwise, right sides together. Sew around the three raw edges leaving an opening 1" (2.5 cm). Through this opening, turn the pocket right side out. Close the opening with a couple of hand stitches.

Place the pocket on the robe wherever you desire with the folded edge on top. Sew the pocket on around the three edges using a straight stitch.

When you are using heavier or quilted material, you should not use the above procedure as the pocket will be too bulky. We suggest that you use a single thickness of fabric. Cut the fabric for the pocket approximately 7¼" (18.5 cm) wide and 8" (20.5 cm) long.

If necessary, overcast the edges all the way around. Fold the top edge 1" (2.5 cm) to the right side; sew the side edges of this facing using a ½" (1.3 cm) seam allowance. Turn the facing to the wrong side.

Pin the pockets to the robe wherever desired. Fold the edges of the pockets under ½" (1.3 cm) and sew three edges to the robe by topstitching.

If you are constructing a rounded pocket, it is easier to press the seam allowances under if you follow this procedure.

Fold the top of the pocket on the folding line to the right side and stitch each side the width of the facing. Continue stitching all the way around the pocket ½" (1.3 cm) from the edge. Turn the facing to the wrong side and press.

For ease in turning the seam allowances of the pocket to the wrong side, machine baste curved edges of the pocket ¼" (6 mm) from the edge. Fold the seam allowances of the pocket to the wrong side along the stitching line, pull up the gathering stitches to ease seam allowance. Press.

Pin the pocket to the front at the position desired. Topstitch the sides and the bottom edge of the pocket to the front, close to the edges.

TIE BELT AND BELT LOOPS:

If you plan to have a tie belt, you can make it as wide and as long as you wish. The length of the belt should be approximately your waist measurement plus 40'' (102 cm). The ends of the belt can be finished at an angle or straight across. If the belt is cut in two pieces, sew the center back seam. Fold the belt double lengthwise, right sides together, and sew the ends and the long edge, leaving an opening for turning. Turn the belt right side out and press it. Close the opening.

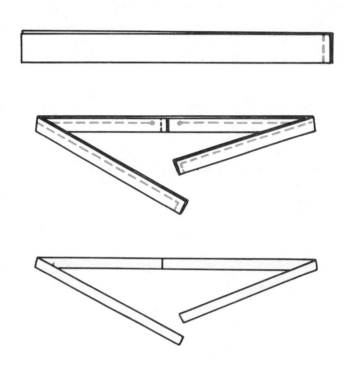

The belt can be placed either underneath the bust or at the waistline. To keep the belt in place, we suggest that you make belt loops. For the loops, cut a strip of fabric 2'' (5 cm) longer than twice the width of the belt. The belt loop can be either wide or narrow. This is a matter of personal preference. We suggest that you attach the loops to the back before you sew the side seams.

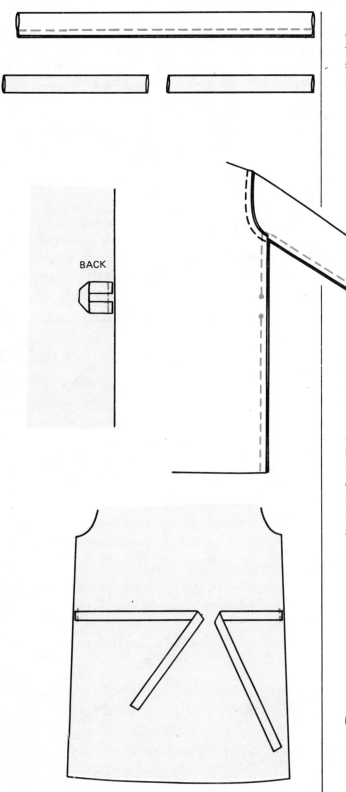

Fold the belt loop double lengthwise, right sides together, and sew the long edge. Turn right side out and press. Cut the loop in two equal lengths. Pin each loop at the side seam with the raw edges together. Secure the ends of the loops with a few stitches.

If you wish to have a tie belt and only tie it in the front, leave an opening on each side seam when you are sewing the side seams. The openings should be the width of the belt. The belt goes through the holes. It is on the inside of the back of the robe and ties in front.

Another variation for the tie belt is to have the belt in two pieces and have the belt sewn to the side seams, then the belt can be tied either in the front or back. Cut two pieces of fabric for the belt twice as wide as you wish the finished belt to be, plus the seam allowances. The length of each belt should be one-fourth of your waist measurement plus approximately 22″ (56 cm) for tieing.

Fold each belt double lengthwise, right sides together, and stitch the long edge and one end. Trim the corners. Turn right side out and press. Attach the belt to the side seams of the back at the waist before you sew the front to the back.

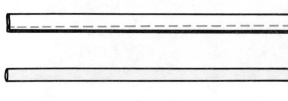

143

APPLIQUE:

An applique is much easier to apply than most people think. They do not take much time and the addition of a design, initials, etc. adds a great deal to a robe. An applique can be placed almost anyplace; on the front and back, yoke, sleeve, or wherever else you desire to place it. You can either make your own applique design or you can use a ready-made design. If you make it yourself, trace off your design and cut it out.

Press a piece of lightweight interfacing on the wrong side of the fabric to be used for the applique. Cut out the applique. Transfer the detail lines to the cut out applique. If you are applying the applique to a garment made from stretch fabric, you should stabilize the fabric under the applique. Place a piece of woven fabric on the wrong side of the garment under the position of the applique and baste it in place by hand.

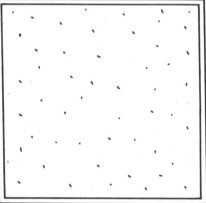

Pin the applique to the garment. It is easier to fuse the applique to the garment. Use a piece of fusible webbing, place it between the applique and garment and press. Stitch over all the raw edges of the applique, use a medium zigzag stitch and a very close stitch length. Add any additional stitching needed to outline the details of the applique.

odds
and
ends

When sewing with ordinary materials it is often very difficult to use up the odds and ends of fabric which are left over. This is not true with lingerie material. There are a great many ways in which these leftover materials may be used. You can give a personal touch to a nightgown or peignoir by adding a rose or a flower; the fabric may be used for small gift items such as matching bonnet or curler bag. A few of the other items that make use of leftover fabric are hair-do saver, slippers, windscarf and smoke-ring.

ROSE:

A beautiful rose is very easy to construct and makes an extremely attractive addition to a pair of slippers. It may also be added to a nightgown or peignoir. The rose may be made from the same color fabric as the basic garment, or you may obtain a very interesting effect by using a contrasting color.

Roses may be made in a variety of sizes and the size depends upon the length and width of the fabric you are using. For a rose large enough to decorate a pair of slippers, use a strip of nylon sheer approximately 5" (13 cm) wide and 24" (61 cm) long. Cut this strip across the grain. Fold the strip, wrong sides together, lengthwise.

Before sewing, trim the ends to form part of a curve as illustrated.

Sew a gathering stitch either by hand or machine using ¼" (6 mm) seam allowance from the raw edges.

Gather the strip by pulling on one of the threads. The tighter you gather, the fuller the rose will be. If you wish to have a rose bud instead of a rose, gather the fabric less.

To form the rose, roll the strip starting at one end. Sew a couple of stitches by hand as you go until you obtain the desired size and shape of the rose. When you obtain the desired size, cut off the excess fabric. Fold the end under and secure with a few stitches by hand.

To cover the raw edges of the rose and at the same time to obtain a neater finish, cut two small circles of nylon sheer large enough to cover the raw edges. Place both circles over the raw edges. Fold under the seam allowance and sew by hand around the circle.

RIBBON FLOWER:

A flower may be made from ribbon. The ribbon should have the same finish on both sides. You can use any width of ribbon, but bear in mind that the greater the width of ribbon, the larger the flower will be.

Fold the ribbon in a zigzag fashion and secure the folds on one side with a gathering stitch. Be sure that you use a strong thread as you have to pull this thread in order to form the flower.

To form the flower, roll the ribbon and secure each roll with a few hand stitches. Remember that the end of the ribbon should be pointed towards the bottom of the flower so that the end will not show when the flower is finished.

Finish the bottom of the flower by using the same technique as used for the bottom of a rose.

DAISY:

A daisy makes a very interesting decoration and is simple to make. Cut a long strip of nylon sheer across the grain approximately 2" (5 cm) wide. The length of the strip determines the number and size of the individual petals on the daisy. If you wish to make a large flower with a lot of petals, make the strip longer. Fold the strip lengthwise, right side to right side, make a small zigzag seam ¼" (6 mm) from the folded edge. Do not trim the seam allowance as it will add color and body to the flower. Turn the strip following the instructions given in Section 2.

After you have turned the strip, make a loop the same size as the petal you wish to have. Secure with a few hand stitches at the center. Repeat this procedure with as many petals as you wish to have.

To cover up the stitches and to finish the center of the flower, wind a portion of the rolled strip very tightly into a small circle. Secure the strip with a few stitches as you form the circle to hold it in place. When you have reached the desired size, secure the end to the wrong side with a few hand stitches.

Attach the circle to the center of the daisy. If you wish you may make the center from a piece of contrasting fabric. This looks more like a real daisy.

POMPOM FLOWER:

This is another flower variation which you may wish to try. Use nylon sheer either in one solid color or in a mixture of colors for a very interesting effect.

Cut the illustrated pattern out of cardboard. The fabric is wound around it to form the flower. Be sure to cut out the center as this is where the flower is tied. Use a wider piece of cardboard if you wish to make a larger flower.

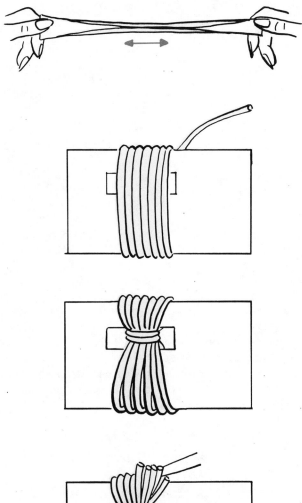

Cut a long strip of nylon sheer ½" (1.3 cm) wide along the grain. Stretch the strip so that the strip becomes a narrow roll.

Wrap the strip around the cardboard winder. The more fabric you wind, the fuller the pompom will be.

Tie the center of the strips securely through the opening in the cardboard. For this use a strip of nylon approximately 5" (13 cm) long and ½" (1.3 cm) wide.

Cut the loops at both ends and remove pompom from the winder.

Fluff up the ends to help form the flower.

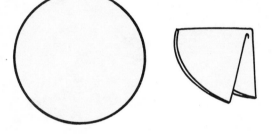

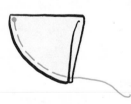

LEAVES:

A leaf helps to show off a flower. They are very easy to make and can be made the same color as the flower, or you may use a contrasting color.

Cut a circle of nylon sheer, the diameter of the circle will be twice the size of the leaf. For a 2-½" (6 cm) leaf, use a 5" (12 cm) circle.

Fold the circle in quarters.

Sew a gathering stitch on the raw edges and then gather to form the leaf. Secure the gathers at the raw edges with a few hand stitches.

You can use as many leaves as you wish for each flower. Either attach them to the bottom of the flower, or attach them directly on the garment where the flower will be placed. You may also make a flower from the leaves by arranging them in a circular fashion and attaching them together in the center. Use the same procedure for covering the center as is used for the center of the daisy.

SLIPPERS:

It is almost impossible to buy a pair of slippers in a store to match a nightgown or peignoir. However, it is a simple matter for the home sewer to make a pair as she can make them from the same fabric as the garment. It does not take very long to make a pair and they can be either plain or fancy. Slippers can be made from any fabric, quilted, nylon tricot, fleece, cotton, corduroy, etc.

150

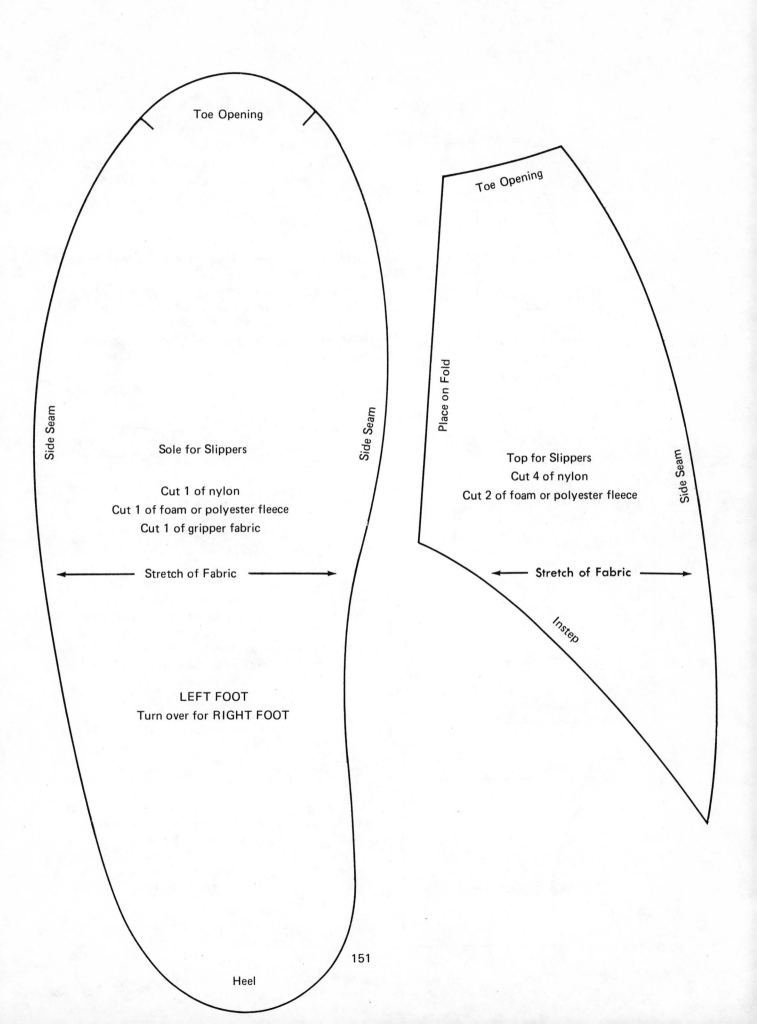

Toe Opening

Side Seam

Side Seam

Sole for Slippers

Cut 1 of nylon
Cut 1 of foam or polyester fleece
Cut 1 of gripper fabric

← Stretch of Fabric →

LEFT FOOT
Turn over for RIGHT FOOT

Heel

151

Toe Opening

Place on Fold

Side Seam

Top for Slippers
Cut 4 of nylon
Cut 2 of foam or polyester fleece

← Stretch of Fabric →

Instep

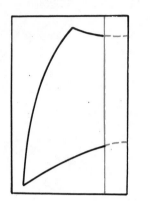

Trace the pattern and then place your foot on the pattern. Make any needed adjustments so that you have the correct size. If you make the sole wider, it is also necessary to increase the width of the top. This should be done on the fold.

We do not recommend nylon for the bottom of the sole as it is too slippery. Almost any other material will be suitable. A baby's lap pad makes excellent soles. Use nylon tricot for the top of the sole and, for softness, use foam or padding between the top and bottom layers. Place the three layers on top of each other with the foam or padding in the middle.

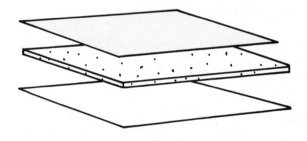

Place the pattern piece on the fabric and trace around the pattern; flip over the pattern piece and mark for the other foot. You have to end up with a left and a right foot pattern. Before you cut out the sole, sew a seam using a straight stitch all the way around where you marked the pattern. This makes it easier, as the fabric has a tendency to move when you are sewing through three layers. Now, cut out the soles, cutting approximately ¼" (6 mm) from the stitches.

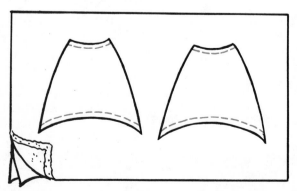

For the top of the slippers, place two pieces of nylon right side to right side. On top of this, place a layer of foam or padding. Place the pattern on the fabric and trace around it. Before you cut out the top, sew a seam on both the toe and the instep leaving the sides open. Cut out the top approximately ¼" (6 mm) from the stitches.

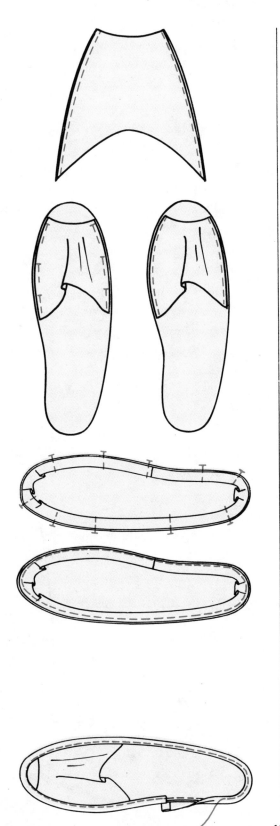

Turn right side out so that the foam is between the nylon layers. So that it will be easier to attach the top to the sole, sew a seam on each side.

Pin the tops to the soles, starting at the mark on the pattern piece. Now try on the slipper and make any necessary adjustments. Sew the top to the sole using a narrow seam allowance.

Cut two 2-½" (6 cm) wide strips, across the grain, and long enough to go around each slipper. Fold each strip double lengthwise, wrong sides together. Pin the strip to the bottom of the sole, raw edges together. Try to start at the inside center of the slipper as this will tend to hide the joining point. Tuck under the end of the strip to make a neat finish. Sew all around the bottom of the sole using a ¼" (6 mm) seam allowance.

Fold the strip to the top of the slipper and topstitch all around.

If you prefer you can use bias tape to cover the raw edges of the slippers.

153

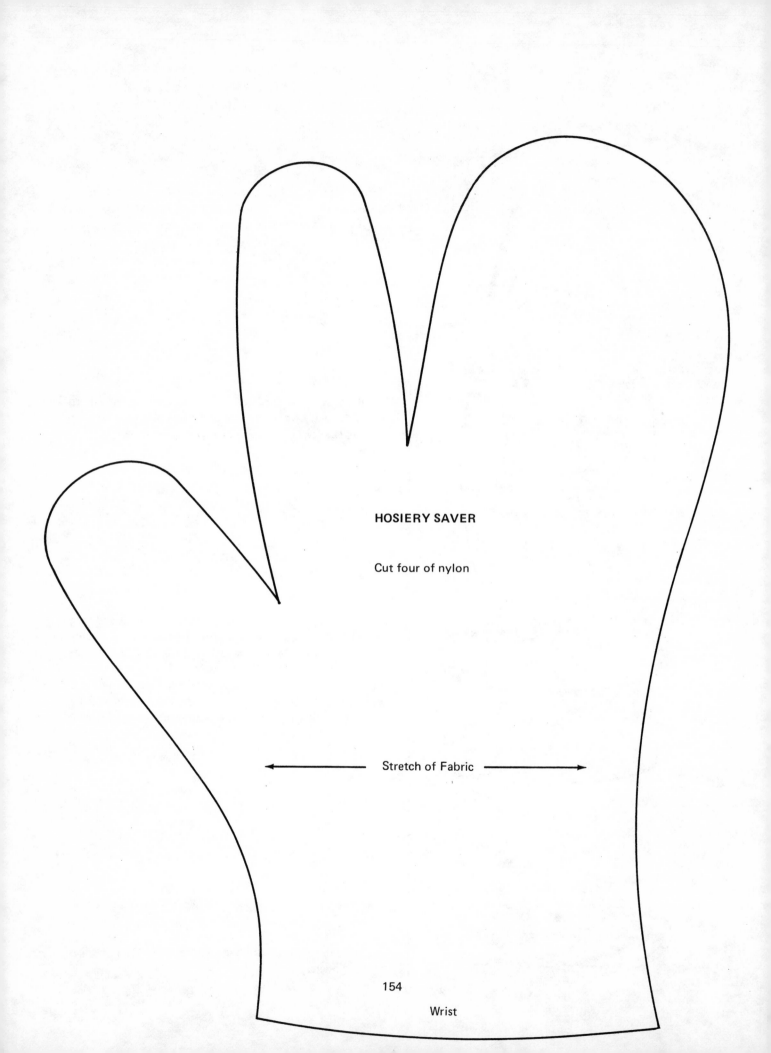

HOSIERY SAVER

Cut four of nylon

←———— Stretch of Fabric ————→

154

Wrist

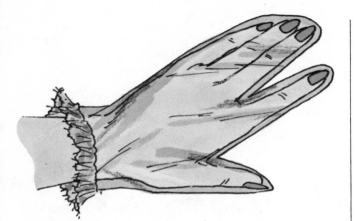

HOSIERY SAVERS:

Hosiery savers cost you only a few pennies to make, yet they can save many dollars if you use them when washing or putting on your nylons. We recommend you use nylon sheer and soft nylon lace approximately ½'' (1.3 cm) wide for the wrist trim. The pattern piece is the same for the left and right hands.

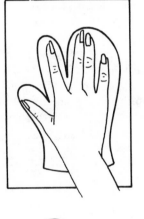

Before cutting, place your hand on the pattern to check your size. Revise the pattern if necessary. Remember to allow enough room for your hand to work freely and for the seam allowance which is 1/8'' (3 mm). Place four layers of fabric on top of each other and cut all four layers at the same time.

For each hand, place right sides together and sew a seam about 2'' (5 cm) up the thumb side. This step will simplify attaching the lace.

Cut two strips of lace approximately 12'' (30 cm) long. Gather the top edge of the lace slightly to fit the wrist opening. An easy way to do this is to pull one thread at the straight edge of the lace to desired fullness.

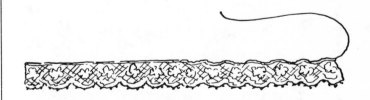

On the wrist opening, overlap the gathered edge of lace about ¼'' (6 mm) from the wrist opening on the right side of fabric. Sew on the lace with a narrow zigzag stitch. Trim away the excess tricot on the wrong side.

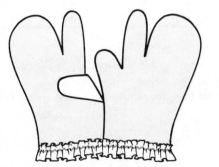

155

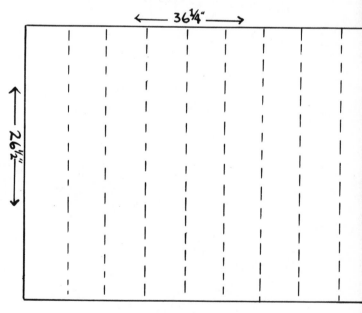

Place the hosiery saver right side to right side and sew all the way around including the lace edge and turn to right side.

BOUFFANT CURLER BONNET:

A curler bonnet is a very useful item to cover hair rollers which do not look very attractive. This bonnet is large enough to go over the largest rollers. Curler bonnets are usually made from nylon sheer. For an extra touch, you may want to place a nylon rose at the top.

Cut out a piece of fabric 26-½" (67 cm) long and 36-¼" (91 cm) wide across the grain. Mark eight vertical lines 4" (10 cm) apart on the wrong side of the fabric. Start marking the first line 4-1/8" (10.5 cm) from the edge to allow for the seam allowance.

Cut nine lengths of 1/8" (3 mm) wide elastic, 11" (28 cm) long. Sew on the elastic to the wrong side of the fabric on each marked line, stretching the elastic to equal the length of fabric.

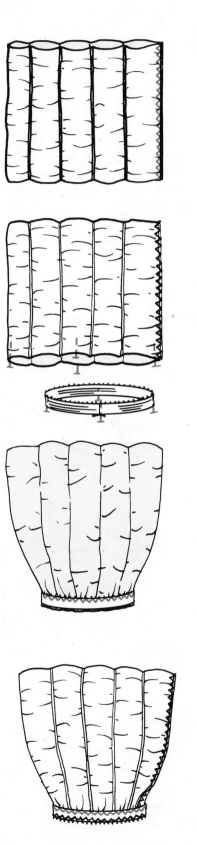

Fold the fabric double, right sides together, and sew a seam on the end. On the wrong side of this seam, sew the last length of elastic.

There are two techniques for applying elastic: one for lingerie elastic, one for narrow elastic with lace. Cut a length of lingerie elastic 17" (43 cm) long. Sew the ends securely together to form a circle; divide the elastic circle and the bottom of curler bonnet in fourths with pins.

Place the elastic circle on the right side of bottom of curler bonnet, matching the pins, with the ruffled edge of elastic facing top of bonnet. Sew a seam just inside the ruffled edge, stretching the elastic between the pins. Trim the excess fabric close to the stitches.

Fold the elastic to wrong side, sew another seam on the straight edge of the elastic, again stretching the elastic to fit the fabric.

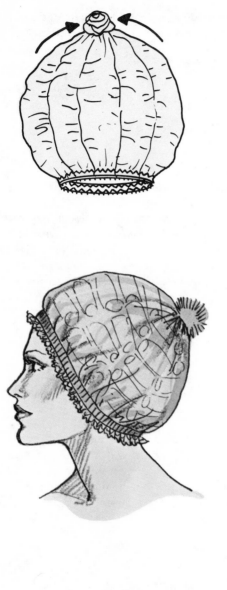

The technique for using narrow elastic and lace edging is as follows: Cut a length of 1/8″ (3 mm) wide elastic 17″ (43 cm) long. Sew the ends securely together to form a circle and divide in fourths with pins. Cut a strip of lace 36″ (91.5 cm) long and sew the ends together to form a circle. Divide the lace circle and bottom of curler bonnet in fourths with pins. Place the elastic circle on the right side of bottom of curler bonnet, matching the pins. Place straight edge of lace circle over the elastic (seam allowance facing down) and sew a medium zigzag stitch through all three thicknesses (nylon, elastic, lace), stretching the elastic between the pins. If you prefer, complete the above technique in two steps: first sew elastic to bonnet, then sew on the lace. Trim the excess nylon close to stitches.

To finish the top of the curler bonnet, sew all nine ends of elastic together, on wrong side. Place a decoration on top if desired.

PLAIN CURLER BONNET:

For a plain curler bonnet, cut a large circle of nylon sheer approximately 21″ (54 cm) in diameter.

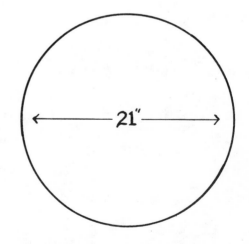

←———— 21″ ————→

Sew a gathering stitch around the outside of the circle using ¼″ (6 mm) seam allowance. Gather the circle slightly.

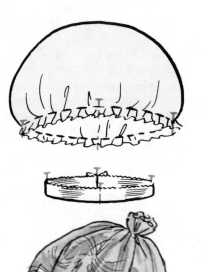

Cut a length of lingerie elastic 17" (43 cm) long. Sew the ends of the elastic together to form a circle. Divide both the elastic and the circle into fourths with pins. Now follow the same procedure as used for sewing on the elastic for a bouffant curler bonnet.

HAIR-DO SAVER:

A hair-do saver is an extremely useful item and it takes only a few minutes to make. Although it is called a hair-do saver, most women use them to cover their faces so that they do not get cosmetics on their clothing. Also, it does protect your hair when you are getting dressed.

Cut a piece of nylon sheer approximately 30" (76 cm) by 15" (38 cm). Follow the instructions on the illustration for cutting out the pattern. Remember that the most stretch goes around your head.

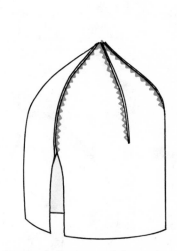

Sew the peaks together starting at the bottom of the peaks to form the top. Sew 2 to 2, 3 to 3, etc. sewing line 1 to 1 last. Do not sew down the center front.

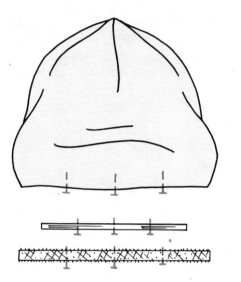

To finish the neckline, cut a length of 1/8" (3 mm) wide elastic 14" (36 cm) long. Cut a strip of narrow lace as long as the neckline. Divide the elastic length in fourths with pins: divide the neckline in fourths with pins. Place the elastic on the right side of neckline, matching the pins. Place the lace over the elastic and sew a medium zigzag seam through all three layers, stretching the elastic between the pins. If you prefer, you may finish the neckline in two steps: first sew the elastic, then sew on the lace. Trim the excess nylon close to the stitches.

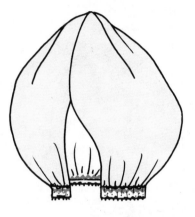

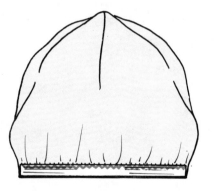

Another way to finish the neckline is to use lingerie elastic. Cut a length of elastic 14" (36 cm) long. Divide the elastic in fourths with pins; divide the neckline in fourths with pins. Pin the elastic to the right side of neckline, matching the pins, with ruffled edge of elastic facing the top of the hair-do saver. Sew seam on the elastic next to the ruffled edge, stretching the elastic as you sew to fit the neckline. Trim the excess fabric close to the stitches.

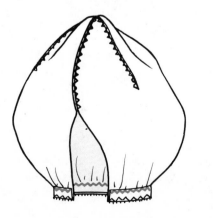

Turn the elastic to the wrong side. Sew another seam on the other edge of the elastic, stretching the elastic as you sew.

Finish the center front edge by folding a narrow seam allowance to the wrong side. Hem with a narrow zigzag seam as close as possible to the fold and trim the excess; if you have a straight stitch machine, fold the raw edge under to form a hem and topstitch.

At center front, turn under the ends of elastic and attach snaps.

WIND BONNET:

A wind bonnet is useful all year long; you never know when a sudden wind will come up and you have to protect your hairdo.

Use a piece of nylon sheer 27″ (68 cm) wide and 18″ (46 cm) long. Fold the fabric double and cut out the pattern with a curved edge as illustrated.

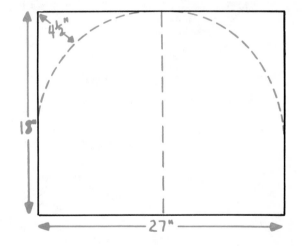

Finish the front edge of the bonnet by folding the edge under 3/8″ (1 cm) to the wrong side. If you have a zigzag machine, sew a narrow zigzag stitch on the edge of the fold and trim the excess fabric.

With a straight stitch machine, fold the edge twice to sew the finished hem.

If you can sew a blindstitch on your sewing machine, sew this seam to get a scalloped finish.

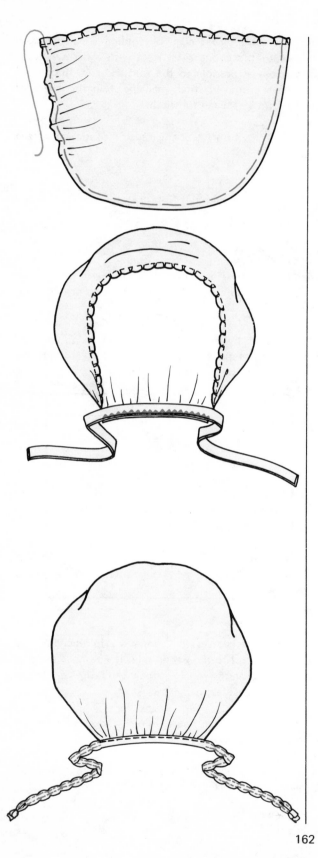

Sew a gathering stitch on the curved neckline by using a long straight stitch with a loose thread tension. Pull the bobbin thread and gather the neckline to approximately 13" (33 cm).

Cut a piece of fabric 42" (107 cm) long and 2" (5 cm) wide for the neckband. Fold this strip of fabric double lengthwise, wrong sides together. Sew the folded neckband on the wrong side of the gathered neckline, raw edges together, using a ¼" (6 mm) seam allowance.

Fold the neckband over the raw edges to the right side and topstitch. Fold in the raw edges of the tie-ends of the neckband and topstitch to finish.

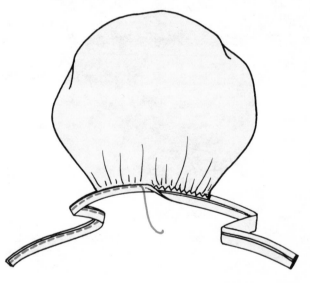

If your machine can sew a blindstitch, sew this seam on both edges of the band to get a scalloped finish.

Tie a tight knot on the ends of the neckband and cut off the excess fabric.

WINDSCARF:

A windscarf is such a versatile item that you can wear it to the opera or to the supermarket. It goes with everything — a long mink coat or a pair of slacks. You will probably wish to make many in a variety of colors.

You need a piece of nylon sheer 66" (168 cm) wide and 17" (43 cm) long. Fold the fabric double, lengthwise. Cut out the shape of the windscarf as illustrated. Mark the back pleats.

Fold and pin the pleats toward the center back. Secure the pleats by sewing a seam ¼" (6 mm) from the raw edge.

Finish the edge of the windscarf by sewing a hem in any one of the following ways all the way around the scarf. Fold the edge under ¼" (6 mm) to the wrong side and sew a narrow zigzag seam on the folded edge. Trim the excess fabric from the wrong side.

If you have a straight stitch machine, fold the edge under twice and hem with a straight stitch.

If you can sew a blind stitch on your machine, use this stitch to obtain a scalloped edge.

SMOKE RING:

There is something very feminine about a smoke ring — that sheer wisp of nylon sheer draped loosely around the neck can do wonders for what would otherwise be an ordinary outfit. Not only do they add a touch of softness, but they also present a wonderful opportunity to experiment with color. Do you look best in a contrasting color? How about a light pastel with a dark dress? Make yourself a dozen in different colors and you will be amazed at how they multiply your wardrobe.

For a smoke ring, you need a piece of fabric 44" (112 cm) long and 20" (52 cm) wide. Cut out the smoke ring on the bias according to the illustration. The finished smoke ring will be 8" (20 cm) wide and 27" (68 cm) around.

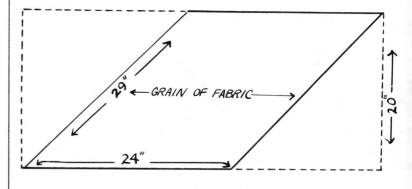

Place the right sides together and sew the angled ends to form a circle, do not turn the smoke ring inside out.

Fold the smoke ring double so that all the raw edges are together.

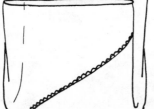

164

Place the top and bottom layers together and begin sewing a seam. Be sure not to catch the two inner layers as they have to move freely. As you sew, pull the two inner layers towards you and sew all the way around the smoke ring to within 1" (2.5 cm) of where you started.

Turn the smoke ring right side out through the opening. Close the opening with a few hand stitches.

SASH:

No woman ever has enough sashes. These items can be used in such an endless variety of ways that you always seem to need one in just a little different shade. A sash always adds a touch of color to make a plain dress something special.

Cut a straight piece of fabric 68" (173 cm) long and 12" (31 cm) wide. Fold the fabric double lengthwise, right side to right side. Cut an angle at each end as illustrated. Sew a seam around the raw edge leaving a 1" (2.5 cm) opening in the middle for turning. Turn the sash rightside out through this opening and close the opening with a few hand stitches.

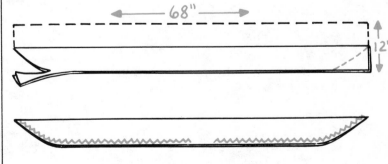

MAKE-UP CAPE:

A make-up cape is not only useful when applying make-up, it can also be used when combing your hair.

Cut out a piece of fabric 28″ (71 cm) long and 28″ (71 cm) wide. Fold the fabric into quarters. Cut out the pattern as illustrated.

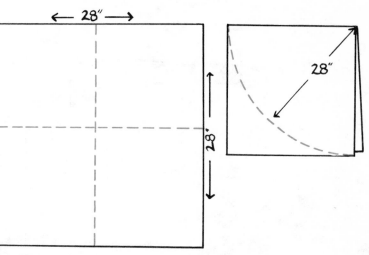

At the point, make a circular cut 2¼″ (6 cm) from the point.

Open the fabric so that it is double. Cut off one folded edge as illustrated.

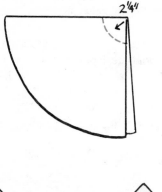

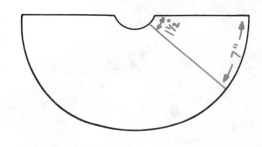

Try on the cape to make sure the opening is large enough. If not, trim the neck opening. If the opening is too large, gather the neckline to the correct size.

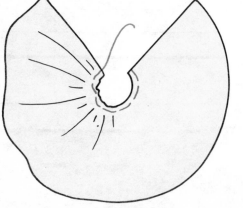

166

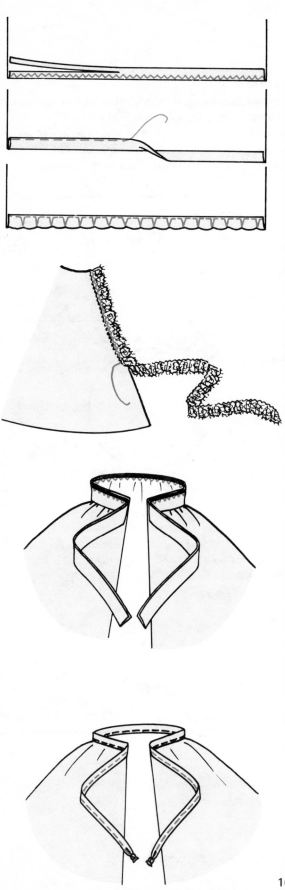

Hem the center front and bottom of the cape by using any of the following techniques. Fold the edge under ¼" (6 mm) to the wrong side and sew a narrow zigzag seam on the folded edge. Trim the excess fabric from the wrong side. If you have a straight stitch machine, fold the edge under twice and hem with a straight stitch. If you can sew a blind-stitch on your sewing machine, use this stitch to obtain a scalloped edge.

If you would like to have lace trim on the edge of your make-up cape, place narrow lace on the right side of the fabric, overlapping the edge ¼" (6 mm). Sew a zigzag seam on the edge of the lace and trim from the wrong side close to the stitches.

Cut a strip of fabric 42" (107 cm) long and 2" (5 cm) wide; this is for the neckband. Fold the neckband double lengthwise, with the wrong sides together. Line up the middle of the neckband with the center back of the cape. Pin the neckband to the wrong side of the neck opening with the raw edges together. Sew a seam using ¼" (6 mm) seam allowance.

Fold the neckband over the raw edges to the right side and topstitch.

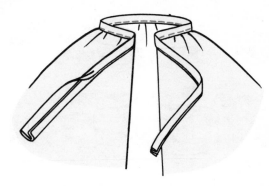

Fold in the raw edges of the tie-ends of the neckband; topstitch to finish. Tie a tight knot on the ends of the neckband and cut off the excess fabric.

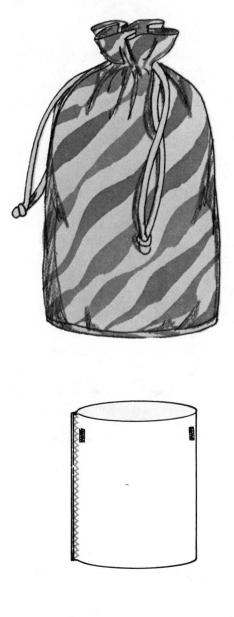

ROLLER BAG:

A roller bag may be made of any material, but heavy nylon tends to work best. Cut out a piece of fabric 11¾″ (30 cm) long and 24″ (61 cm) wide. Cut out two circles of the same fabric with a diameter of 8″ (20 cm). Cut out a piece of firm material such as foam using the same diameter.

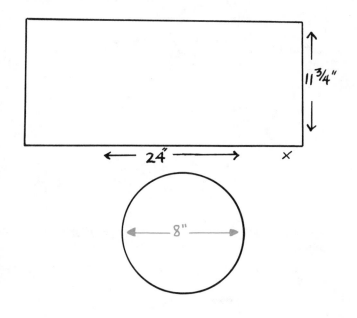

Fold the long fabric piece double, right sides together, and sew the side seam. Make a buttonhole on each side of the roller bag, starting 2¾″ (7 cm) from the top. These buttonholes are for the drawstring.

Fold the top of the opening 2″ (5 cm) to the wrong side, all around the top of the bag. Fold the raw edge under ½″ (1.3 cm) and sew a seam on the fold.

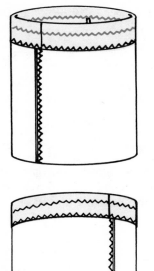

Sew a second seam ¾" (2 cm) from the first seam.

Place the foam rubber circle between the nylon pieces and sew a seam around the circle (through all three layers).

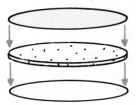

Pin the circle to the bottom of the roller bag, right sides together. Sew the raw edges together using ¼" (6 mm) seam allowance. For a neater finish, overcast the seam allowance with a zigzag stitch.

For the drawstring, cut two 25" (63 cm) long bands. Thread these bands through the buttonholes, pull one band through each buttonhole, sew the ends of each band together, or make a knot, to form two circles inside the casing.

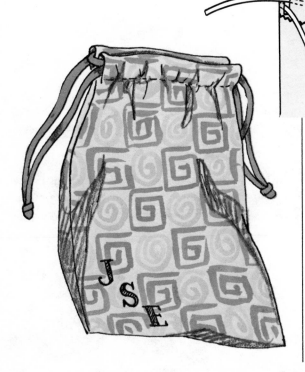

SHOE BAG:

A shoe bag is very handy for anyone who travels. It keeps the rest of your clothing from getting soiled from dirty shoes and, in addition, it makes it easier to pack your bags. This makes a wonderful gift item for friends who travel, you can decorate it with an applique or an initial. You can make them in various sizes. Larger ones are good for soiled laundry and a small one is excellent for a lavender bag for your lingerie drawer.

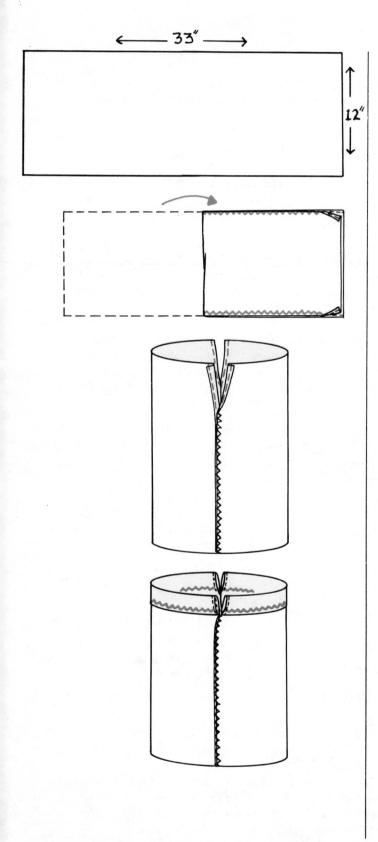

For a shoe bag, cut a piece of fabric 12″ (30 cm) wide and 33″ (84 cm) long.

Fold the fabric double lengthwise, right sides together. Sew the side seams starting 2″ (5 cm) from the top. At the top of the side seams, hem the raw edges by turning ¼″ (6 mm) to the wrong side.

Fold the top opening over to the wrong side 1″ (2.5 cm), fold under the raw edge and hem around the opening.

Cut two strings 25″ (30 cm) long. Insert the strings in the hem following the same procedure as used for the curler bag.